feeding
your baby

feeding your baby

Dr Penny Stanway and Sara Lewis

hamlyn

First published in 2005 by Hamlyn,
a division of Octopus Publishing Group Ltd
2–4 Heron Quays London E14 4JP

ISBN-13: 978-0-600-61289-6
ISBN-10: 0-600-61289-9

A CIP catalogue record for this book is
available from the British Library

Printed and bound in China

10 9 8 7 6 5 4 3

notes

Standard level spoon measures are used in all
recipes:

   1 tablespoon = one 15 ml spoon
   1 teaspoon = one 5 ml spoon

Ideally stock should be freshly made; see recipes
on page 126. Alternatively, buy a carton of fresh
stock, ensuring it is free from added salt for
under-ones.

Use full-fat milk unless otherwise specified.
Medium eggs should be used unless otherwise
specified.

A few recipes include nuts and nut derivatives.
Anyone with a known nut allergy must avoid these.
Children under the age of 3 with a family history of
nut allergy, eczema or any other type of allergy are
also advised to avoid eating dishes which contain
nuts. Do not give whole nuts or seeds to any child
under 5 because of the risk of choking.

contents

introduction

Good food is one of life's great pleasures – it's also vital for good health. So, one of our most important roles as parents is to give our children a variety of food they'll enjoy and that will help them grow up healthy.

From a growing baby to a toddler, and beyond, a well-balanced diet has enough nutrients and calories to meet a child's needs. It lays the foundation of a lifetime of good health, and helps your child stay fit and full of energy.

Giving your child a nutritious diet can, however, prove to be a challenge. Initially, as a first-time mum, you have to learn when and how to introduce 'solids', what to offer, and how to ease your baby's progress towards eating the same food as the rest of your family. Secondly, you may have a toddler or young child who is fussy about food. Thirdly, we are all subject to media food scares, questioning which foods really are good for us. And lastly, as role models to our children, we may need to improve our own eating habits before we can guide our children towards a healthy diet.

For the first six months breast (or formula) milk will provide everything that your baby requires to stay healthy, but from six months she will require additional foods to supplement her changing nutritional needs. The time when your child starts to eat solids is a period of great discovery, but give your baby time to adjust to this new way of receiving nourishment, especially in the first few weeks of weaning.

The foundations for adult food preferences are laid down during a child's first two years and many children find it hard later to accept types of food that are not offered at this time. 'Nursery food' always has a certain appeal to young children, but it is most important to offer your child an interesting and varied diet that includes plenty of fruit and vegetables, mixed grains, milk and dairy products,

eggs, pulses, nuts and seeds and either meat, fish or soya-rich products.

It is also important to realize that feeding your family well will reduce their risk of certain illnesses not only when they are children but when they are grown up too. This is partly because healthy eating habits learnt now will probably stay with them in adult life. And having a healthy diet as an adult is proven to reduce the risk of problems such as adult-onset diabetes, several sorts of cancer, gum disease, osteoporosis and arterial disease.

Once weaning is well established, your baby's diet can quickly broaden and there are lots of recipes in this book to tempt her. Initially she will start by eating simple vegetable purées, but she will rapidly be able to try a range of tastes and textures, such as Tuna Ragu (see page 66) or Mini

Mealtimes are an central part of family life.

Apple Custard Pots (see page 72), both of which are suitable from the age of nine months. By the time she is approaching her first birthday, your feeding routine should be well established, and as she becomes a toddler you will be able to share an increasing number of family meals, such as Chicken Casserole (see page 84) or Fruit Crumble (see page 111).

This book is packed with practical information and advice on everything you need to know about feeding your baby and toddler – from when to begin weaning, and what foods to offer and when, to tips on batch cooking to save time, advice on food safety, allergies and fussy eaters, plus lots of easy yet delicious everyday recipes that your child is very likely to enjoy.

the importance of milk

The best food for a baby is milk, and undoubtedly the best milk is breast milk. Nutritionally, babies need only milk for the first six months, and milk remains the most important part of a baby's diet – even after starting solids – for at least the first year.

BREAST MILK
Breastfeeding gives your baby the best start in life and is the ideal food and drink. It contains all the nutrients he needs in the right proportions, as well as many antibodies, which help fight infections. The high levels of fatty acids also protect a baby susceptible to allergies. Iron levels are low in breast milk, but they are in a readily absorbed form and combine with your baby's iron stores (all babies are born with a store of iron that lasts six months) to provide all his needs for the first six months.

HOW MUCH MILK?
Breastfed babies generally require more milk feeds than bottle-fed babies. A feed can last from 10 minutes to half an hour or more, depending on the individual baby. Bottle-fed babies need about six feeds a day, following the suggested quantities on the formula packet.

There are many other advantages to breastfeeding. Breast milk can adjust if your baby is premature, alter as your baby grows and his needs change and even dilute in hot weather to satisfy his thirst. Breastfeeding is free and the milk is always ready at the right temperature, virtually on demand. The supply never runs out and is ready to satisfy a hungry baby whatever the time, day or night.

FORMULA MILK
The powdered cow's milk used in formula milk is modified to be as close to the nutritional composition of breast milk as possible and is fortified with vitamins and minerals. Whey-based formulas are given to newborn babies, while follow-on milks have a higher proportion of casein to whey and are suited to hungrier babies over six months. Make up formula feeds with previously boiled water and store in the refrigerator until required. Do not use either water that has been repeatedly boiled, or softened water or bottled water, as they can be high in certain mineral salts. Continue with formula milk feeds until your baby is 12 months, then progress to full-fat cow's milk.

Give milk in bottles with teats for babies and always thoroughly clean and sterilize all bottles and equipment between feeds.

SOYA-BASED INFANT FORMULA

You may need to include a soya-based formula in your baby's diet if he develops a lactose intolerance or if you follow a dairy-free vegetarian diet and wish to bring your child up the same way. Whatever the reason, you must seek medical advice before feeding your baby soya milk.

Unlike other milks, soya does not contain sugar and is often sweetened with glucose syrup, which can be detrimental to teeth. Some soya formulas also contain small levels of aluminium and so are unsuitable for premature babies or those suffering from kidney problems. Do not give babies unmodified (or carton) soya milks before they are two years old.

GOAT'S MILK

Goat's milk infant formula is suitable to use from birth. However, like cow's milk formula and soya-based formula, it can cause allergies. Ask your health professional or doctor about 'Nanny' infant formula. Do not give full-fat fresh goat's milk as a main drink to babies until they are over 12 months and then only if it is pasteurized.

COW'S MILK

A good source of energy, protein, vitamins and minerals, cow's milk is especially important for calcium, which is essential for growing teeth and bones. It can be added to cooking from six months, but should not be given as a drink to babies under 12 months of age, as breast milk or formula contain greater quantities of essential vitamins and iron needed for growth.

BREASTFEEDING CHALLENGES

Like any new skill, breastfeeding can be hard to master, especially in the early days. Do persevere if you can and don't be afraid to seek advice from your midwife, health visitor or breastfeeding counsellor. In addition to giving your baby's immune system a head start and providing the nutritional benefits described opposite, the emotional benefits of this natural bond can be very rewarding. Ideally, continue breastfeeding until your baby is at least one year old, and then carry on until you and your baby are ready to stop.

first solids

The introduction of the first baby purées signals the start of a new and exciting landmark in your baby's development, even though milk remains your baby's most important food for the first year.

You should ideally start offering foods other than milk when your baby is six months old, although some babies want 'solids' slightly earlier, in which case you can start weaning at four months. However, never give your child solids before the age of four months without your doctor's approval as your baby's digestive system may be too immature to cope, and it might also increase the likelihood of an allergic reaction.

individual so don't feel pressurized into offering your child solids early on simply because your friends have. It isn't a competition and there are advantages to waiting until six months. Be guided by how you and your baby feel.

In the early days of weaning, the aim is to introduce your baby to the tastes and textures of foods other than milk, not for these new foods to provide lots of extra nourishment.

WHAT IS WEANING?

Weaning is the process of introducing solid foods, and it often begins with giving tiny spoonfuls of smooth baby rice (see box, page 13) or vegetable purée to a baby alongside her usual milk feeds. Gradually, as your baby adapts to feeding from a spoon, the quantity and number of meals can be increased from one mini-meal a day to three. As she progresses, so the purée can become thicker and coarser, until, after a number of months, she can eat a finely chopped version of the family's meal.

Knowing what foods and when to give them when weaning are crucial. Some babies relish this new stage, while others prefer to wait. Some like the same food over and over again, while others are happy to try new tastes and quickly move on to more varied purées. Each baby is an

HOW TO WEAN

To introduce solids, continue with your usual milk feeds but choose a time of day, such as lunchtime, to offer a spoonful or so of one of the first foods (see pages 12 and 26–43), after some milk.

Two weeks later, offer solids at another time of day, such as breakfast, and gradually build up to two and then three mini-meals a day over the next four to six weeks, adapting the quantities to suit her appetite. Keep flavours mild and very simple and make sure purées are slightly sloppy and lump-free.

You can offer solids for breakfast, lunch and supper, or for a snack mid-morning and at teatime. Babies vary hugely in how much, and how often they want solids. With time, you can become more adventurous by combining flavours, making purées thicker and coarser, and adding meat in the form of chicken or turkey. Maintain breastfeeds or aim for 600 ml (1 pint) infant formula milk a day.

FEEDING THE FIRST SOLIDS

Give your baby some breast milk or formula first, then offer a little taste from a shallow teaspoon – or even from your (washed) finger. If your baby likes it, give a little more. Do the same for each new food. Be sensitive to your baby's appetite and let her guide you as to how much to give. Finish with another drink of milk.

Put the laden spoon into your baby's mouth, then gently withdraw it against the upper gum and lip so some of the food stays in the mouth. Your baby may try to suck in some of the food from the spoon. Some inquisitive six-month-olds like to investigate by grasping food from their mother's hand or plate. This is fine as long as it's suitable and not too hot.

Many babies love the new sensations of smelling, tasting and swallowing solids – they smack their lips and start looking for more at once – but the experience takes others by surprise. A screwed-up face doesn't mean your baby doesn't like the food, just that it's unfamiliar. So simply wait for a moment, so your baby doesn't feel pressurized, then have another go. A lot of the food that goes into your baby's mouth will probably come out again, but you can scoop this up gently from the chin with the spoon.

Never add puréed food to a bottle. Doing this would reduce the amount of liquid the baby drinks from that bottle, which could lead to dehydration.

SITTING COMFORTABLY

At first, you and your baby will probably feel happiest if she sits on your lap so that she feels secure. Protect her clothes with a bib or a muslin nappy, and your own with a tea towel. As feeding progresses and your baby grows, a baby's car seat – placed on a secure surface or the floor – may be easier.

Allow plenty of time so that you and your baby can enjoy this new experience. If you have older children, offer your baby solids when the other children are at school or playgroup and the house is peaceful.

INTRODUCING NEW FOODS AND TEXTURES

At first, give your baby relatively runny, soft, smooth purées that she can swallow easily. Once your baby is happily eating smooth 'solids', you can progress quite quickly to thicker, lumpier ones. Babies of this age soon learn to grind soft lumps of food with their gums. From about nine to 12 months, they learn to grind harder lumps with their gums, and as the back teeth emerge, they use these too. However, a lot depends on the type of food and the size of the pieces you give. Meat is difficult to chew, so it needs to be either chopped and blended, or minced, until your baby is around ten months old. After that it may be all right simply cut into very small pieces.

Solids become progressively more important during the second half of the first year for most babies, although milk should still provide most of their nourishment. When the nourishment your baby gets from solids begins to equal that from milk, it's important to ensure that you are providing a good balance of the different food groups, but this doesn't usually happen until about a year at the earliest.

HOMEMADE OR READY-MADE FOOD?

Many mothers like to give their babies homemade food most of the time – especially when they can easily adapt what the rest of the family is eating. It's obviously much cheaper to make your own – and if you adapt family recipes, this means your baby quickly gets used to normal family food. In addition, making your own baby food ensures that you know exactly what has gone into it and guarantees that it is free from any additives.

weaning tips

- Be guided by your baby and health professional as to when to wean

- Learning to eat from a spoon is a tricky skill for a new baby and can be messy

- Never force feed your baby

- Go slowly – try just one new taste at a time in the first few weeks

- Use sterilized equipment up to six months. Continue sterilizing teats and bottles until no longer required

baby rice

PREPARING FIRST TASTES

If you are introducing solids before six months then commercially produced powdered baby rice is probably the easiest first food to offer, as it is simple to prepare and the portions required are so small. The taste won't be too dissimilar to the milk your baby is used to and should be happily received. If she appears distressed, stop and try again in a few days' or weeks' time.

To prepare, mix1 teaspoon of 'pure' baby rice to a smooth, slightly sloppy consistency with breast milk, formula milk, or previously boiled and cooled water (see packet instructions). Check the temperature – it should be just lukewarm – then offer to your baby from a small, rounded, plastic baby spoon.

If your baby enjoyed the rice, offer it again once a day during the next few days to allow time for her digestive system to adapt, then gradually build up to 2–3 teaspoons of food.

3 ways to purée food

• mash

• mouli

• blend

What you do will depend on the food and your equipment. Use a fork or a sieve for vegetables and fruit, or a mouli for larger quantities. The only way of making meat smooth is by blending, but chop it finely first or it will be stringy.

Jars or tins of commercially prepared food are convenient; for example, when you are on a day out, or on holiday. So it's worth keeping a few handy in the cupboard.

BATCH COOKING AND FREEZING

As a baby eats such tiny amounts, especially in the early days of weaning, it can be a great time-saver to make up larger quantities of purée and freeze individual portions for other times; plus it really doesn't take much longer to purée two carrots rather than one.

Make a larger quantity of simple purées, or double baby recipes, then purée or mash. Take out a portion for the next meal and cover and chill in the refrigerator until needed. Spoon the remainder into sections of a sterilized ice cube tray or mini plastic pots. Cool, loosely covered, then seal and label clearly with the date and type of food. Freeze as soon as possible and use within six weeks. If you are using ice cube trays, open freeze until solid, then pop the cubes into a plastic container, seal and label. (Make sure both ice cube trays and containers are sterilized. Use plastic freezer bags from six months.)

When you want to use it, take out one or more frozen cubes as needed (you can use a mix of ice cubes for new flavours), put in a bowl, cover and allow to defrost at room temperature for an hour or so, or overnight in the refrigerator. Alternatively, use the microwave. Always reheat defrosted food thoroughly in a saucepan, or in the microwave, then cool to the correct temperature for your baby.

THINNING PURÉES

Getting the right texture of solids for your child's stage of development is important and it is easier to start with a thicker purée and thin it to the correct consistency. Purée or mash the food, and then add a little of the following if you need to thin it:

- **Expressed breast milk** or **formula**; this makes a new food more tempting because it adds a familiar flavour and a little sweetness
- **Water** in which you've cooked the vegetables or fruit
- **Water** which has been previously boiled and cooled
- For **savoury purées**, add **homemade vegetable stock** (see page 126) or chicken stock (see page 126), conveniently frozen in an ice-cube tray so you can use a cube at a time

DOES YOUR BABY SEEM TO HAVE TROUBLE SWALLOWING?

Try thinning the baby food with extra breast milk or formula, or a little cooled boiled water. Also, try reducing the amount that you put on the spoon. If this doesn't help, abandon the solid meal and give your baby a milk feed with lots of reassuring cuddles. Try again in a few days' time and, if you still have problems, see your health visitor or doctor to check that there is not a more serious reason.

If your baby chokes or gags on lumpy food, adjust the consistency until he or she is a little older.

which foods to introduce when

Knowing what to offer, how much and how often are some of the key issues when starting weaning. Remember that milk is still the most important source of nutrition for your baby and that the new sensations offered at meals are the start of a lifetime of healthy eating.

LIQUIDS

Breastfed babies aged under three to four months do not usually need drinks other than breast milk. Breast milk is such an important source of nourishment even for a baby who has started solids, that you shouldn't give more than a little of any other drink.

From six weeks, offer cooled, boiled water to babies fed on formula milk. Use freshly drawn and boiled water and do not give babies water from a tap fitted with a water softener. Avoid sparkling water or still water with a high mineral content.

As your baby grows, you may want to offer different drinks too, but try to get into the habit of reading labels. Artificial sweeteners, such as aspartame, saccharin or acesulfame-K are not designed for babies. Unsweetened fruit juices may be given to older babies between 9 and 12 months if they are diluted 1 part juice to 10 parts water.

SOLIDS – WHERE TO BEGIN

Baby rice or finely puréed and sieved potato is the best starting point for introducing solids. If your baby seems to enjoy these first few mini-mouthfuls, then move on and try some other tastes, such as puréed vegetables, fruits or porridge. The best first foods are butternut squash, sweet potato, parsnip or carrot, and dessert apples or pears are good fruits to start with. You can then begin combining flavours and gradually adding other vegetables and fruit as well as meat, eggs and pulses. The chart on pages 16–17 gives a breakdown of the different food groups and when to start introducing them into your child's diet.

PICKINESS

Early eating habits may set a pattern for later life, so while it's wise to offer a little of everything, it isn't advisable to make a fuss if a young child doesn't eat something.

carrots

butternut squash

sweet potato

pears

first foods planner

As some babies want to start weaning at four months, the chart below includes foods suitable from that age. If, like most mothers, you start at six months, then start with the foods for four-month-olds and gradually introduce foods from the next age groups when your child is ready.

	VEGETABLES	NON-GLUTEN GRAINS	OTHER STARCHY CARBOHYDRATES	FRUIT
from 4 months	✔ Broccoli ✔ Avocado ✔ Cauliflower ✔ Squash ✔ Courgette ✔ Carrots and other root vegetables	✔ Rice ✔ Corn (e.g. polenta) ✔ Millet	✔ Tapioca ✔ Sago	✔ Apple ✔ Apricots ✔ Banana ✔ Pears
from 5 months		✘ Buckwheat		✘ Melon ✘ Peaches ✘ Plums
from 6 months				✘ Berries ✘ Citrus fruits ✘ Kiwifruit

*   As bread and rusks, breakfast cereals and flour-based sauces.

**   If beans and lentils make your baby windy, give them for lunch rather than supper, so it doesn't affect your baby's night sleep.

*** As long as there is no history of allergies in the family (see pages 22–23).

tips for feeding in the first year

FOOD SAFETY

Note that while true food allergy is rare, it can be serious, and nuts – especially peanuts – are a common trigger.

Don't give whole or chopped nuts, or whole seeds, to a child under five, as there is a risk of inhalation or choking.

DAIRY FOODS (FULL-FAT)	GRAINS THAT CONTAIN GLUTEN	PULSES AND LEGUMES	MEATS AND FISH	NUTS AND SEEDS
✗ None	✗ None	✗ None	✗ None	✗ None
✗ None	✗ None	✗ None	✔ Chicken ✔ Turkey	✗ None
✔ Cow's milk ✔ Cheese ✔ Yogurt ✔ Eggs (well cooked)	✔ Wheat* ✔ Barley* ✔ Rye* ✔ Oats*	✔ Peas (tiny tastes can be given earlier) ✔ Lentils** ✔ Beans** ✔ Tofu	✔ Lamb ✔ Beef ✔ Pork ✔ Filleted fish	✔ Ground nuts*** ✔ Seeds***

- **Space out new first foods** When giving your baby anything other than root vegetables for the first time, don't give it again for four days. You can then see if your baby develops any symptoms – such as diarrhoea, a runny nose or a rash – that suggest an allergy or other sensitivity. It also gives your baby the chance to get used to each new taste.

- **Combining foods** Once a baby is used to single flavours – after the first two or three weeks – try mixtures such as:

  ✔ Carrot and cauliflower   ✔ Squash and beetroot
  ✔ Courgette and parsnip
  ✔ Leek and potato   ✔ Sago and apricot
  ✔ Rice and broccoli   ✔ Pear and semolina

getting the texture right

It is essential to get the consistency of your baby's food suitable for her age and preference. If it is too thick or coarse she will not be able to swallow it. If it is sloppy for too long, she will become a lazy eater.

CONSISTENCY

By the age of about six months, your baby will begin to learn to chew. As she progresses, introduce her to more exciting textures so that she moves from purées to mashed and, later, to chopped foods.

If foods are very liquid for too long, the chewing stage of development may be missed and your child may be reluctant to join in family meals later. However, if chunky solids are introduced too early then your child may gag on the lumps and be put off eating that food.

Teething brings an additional set of challenges. A baby may be reluctant to eat coarser foods if her gums are sore, so wait a few days and then reintroduce them when she is feeling brighter.

from 6–9 months

Begin with a sloppy purée of baby rice or potato. Move on to purées of butternut squash, sweet potato, parsnip or carrot, cooked apple or pear, or thin non-gluten porridge. First foods must be puréed smoothly, but after a few weeks, introduce slightly less smooth purées.

Next, make smooth purées with a slightly thicker texture. Offer new tastes, such as red lentils, avocado and papaya. If your baby is coping brilliantly with smoothly puréed food, offer slightly thicker food for a week or two, then gradually introduce slightly lumpy food, and progress to bigger lumps. If at any stage she splutters or protests over lumpy food, make it a little smoother next time.

Next, give coarser textures. Mashing soft foods – such as cooked carrots and squash – is ideal, as it doesn't get food as smooth as blending or sieving.

Offer first finger foods, such as a cooked broccoli or cauliflower floret or cooked carrot, at eight or nine months.

from 9–12 months

At this stage, you can give your baby a wide variety of coarsely mashed or chopped meals, plus finger foods such as cooked or raw vegetables, fruit or toast fingers, to pick up and eat. Babies enjoy dipping finger foods to combine flavours.

managing fussy eaters

Most children go through a fussy-eating stage at some time, and this can be caused by a number of factors. It may last a day or two, a week or two or even longer as your child gets older.

Children who eat sitting at the table with other people are more likely to eat well and with less fuss. Try to encourage calm, unrushed mealtimes, because this helps digestive juices to flow, and this, in turn, helps the body absorb nutrients.

Fussiness shows up in a number of ways:

DISLIKE OF LUMPY FOODS

Some babies dislike lumpy foods because they've become too used to smooth purées, or because lumpy foods have been introduced too early and they've been put off by choking on a lump (see also page 18).

SPITTING OUT FOOD

Put less food on the spoon so that your baby's mouth isn't full. Check if it is too hot or cold. Mix a new flavour with an equal quantity of something he likes. If you have just begun weaning, change from baby rice to puréed potato. If that isn't successful, perhaps your baby just isn't ready for solids, so wait a week or two, then try again.

PLAYING WITH FOOD

They may not be hungry, perhaps because they've been drinking a lot, or eating too many snacks. Alternatively, they may be ill.

FOOD REFUSAL

Your baby might be more in need of a drink, or he might be too hot or cold.

> **DON'T DESPAIR**
> - Never force a baby to have the last teaspoon in the bowl. He will soon turn his head away when he's had enough
> - No baby will starve himself. Continue offering a variety of foods and don't despair; the food fad will disappear just as quickly as it arrived
> - A baby's appetite can vary from meal to meal and from day to day

A cold wet nappy, teething or a sore bottom could be distracting your baby, or he may simply be testing your limits.

LACK OF APPETITE

If he refuses food that he has tried and liked before, and the problem persists for several days, seek advice from your doctor.

MEAL TIMES ARE A BATTLE OF WILLS

As your child gets older, he will quickly realize that refusing food provokes a reaction. Try to stay calm, explain that if he doesn't want any dinner, that's fine, but there won't be snacks instead. If he is very hungry later, offer a piece of fruit.

Try not to serve only food that you know your child will eat, as this can quickly lead to your having to cook two meals each time.

which foods to avoid

In the first year in particular, there are a number of items that you should avoid completely – particularly added salt and sugar – as they may be detrimental to your child's health.

avoiding salt

Common salty or sodium-rich foods to avoid include:

- Bacon, kippers and other smoked food
- Sausages
- Paté
- Stock cubes
- Yeast extracts, such as Marmite
- Soy sauce
- Tomato ketchup
- Many chutneys and pickled foods
- Many 'ready' meals, including soups, cook-chilled and frozen meals
- Many canned vegetables
- Bicarbonate of soda and baking powder

SALT AND SALTY FOODS

Salt is too 'strong' for a baby's kidneys to process, and at worst they may be unable to get rid of it, which could make them dangerously ill. Therefore do not add any salt to the food you are cooking, especially for children under one. The culprit in salt is the mineral sodium – so under-ones should also avoid non-salty foods that are rich in sodium (see box).

Don't add salt or salty stock cubes when making baby food, but cook baby food in homemade, salt-free chicken or vegetable stock (see page 126), boiled water, formula or full-fat cow's milk.

If your baby is sharing a family meal, add salt to adult portions once his portion has been served; you could also use herbs and spices to give more flavour if necessary. Stock cubes can be used in family meals for babies over nine months, but choose a low-salt brand and always make up with extra water.

SUGAR

The sugar you add to food – rather than the type naturally present in fruits, vegetables and milk – provides 'empty' calories. This means it supplies energy but no other nutrients. Added sugar is best avoided completely for babies of up to nine months. After that, the very occasional (perhaps weekly) helping of food containing added sugar won't hurt. You may, however, prefer to avoid it for as long as possible – until your baby is old enough to realize that he is missing out on something.

Try to avoid adding sugar to foods so that you don't bring up your baby with an overly sweet tooth. Sweeten sharper fruits with naturally sweet ones, such as bananas with plums and ripe pears with a little orange juice. Soak, cook and purée dried apricots or dates and stir into natural yogurt or fromage frais for a delicious dessert. Extremely sharp fruits, such as rhubarb or gooseberries, may require a little sugar to make them palatable, but these are the exceptions and you should encourage your child to enjoy the taste of foods in their natural state.

Always remember to clean your baby or child's teeth and gums after giving any food containing added sugar.

HONEY

Don't give this to children under one as it is high in sugar. Also, there is a tiny risk of food poisoning from a toxin which is very rarely present in unpasteurized honey.

BRAN

Don't give your baby breakfast cereals containing added or concentrated bran, as this could prevent iron, calcium and zinc being properly absorbed. Bran is also very filling, which could spoil your baby's appetite later in the day.

OFFAL

Avoid giving large quantities of liver to a child as vitamin A levels are too high. A tiny portion of puréed or finely chopped well-cooked liver may be served to a baby from six to nine months, once a week, until he is over one year old.

SHELLFISH

As incidents of food poisoning with prawns and mussels are high, it is best to avoid giving shellfish to a child under one year old, and possibly safer to wait until they are over two years old.

SOFT DRINKS

Most drinks marketed for young children are high in sugar, additives and often caffeine. Encourage your child to drink water or diluted fruit juice.

Biscuits contain added sugar.

Honey may contain toxins.

Bran is not suitable for babies.

allergies

Some children are more susceptible than others to an allergic reaction triggered by a particular food. Those most at risk are from families with a history of allergic asthma, eczema or hay fever.

WHO IS SUSCEPTIBLE?

An estimated 1 in 10 children is prone to allergy. Although many grow out of their allergies by the time they are two, others have a sensitivity to nuts, eggs, milk or shellfish for life. The Department of Health recommends that infants who have a strong family history of allergy should be breastfed for at least four months and longer if possible. Weaning should not occur until five or six months and new foods should be introduced one at a time. Seek expert advice before modifying a child's diet or if you feel that there may be something wrong with your baby.

RISKS OF HAVING AN ALLERGY

Your baby has a higher risk of developing an allergy if you, your partner, or a close relative has eczema, allergic asthma, allergic rhinitis (e.g. hay fever), urticaria, or a food allergy. If you are concerned that your baby's risk is high, to reduce it you can:

- **Breastfeed exclusively for six months, and continue to breastfeed for at least the rest of the first year.**

- **While breastfeeding, avoid eating dairy foods, eggs, fish and nuts. Seek advice from your doctor or a dietician, if necessary, on replacing these foods so that your diet remains sound.**

- **Delay giving your baby the following:**
  Cow's milk (and 'unhydrolysed soy' formula) until nine months old
  Wheat until 10 months old
  Eggs until 11 months old
  Cheese, **yogurt**, **oranges**, **fish** and **nuts** until 12 months old
  Peanuts and foods containing **peanut oil** until five years of age

One study found that excluding these foods reduced a baby's risk of allergy from 40 per cent to 14 per cent. However, discuss this eating plan with your doctor before implementing it, and follow it only under the guidance of a doctor or dietician.

When you give one of these foods for the first time, avoid other new foods for the next four days, and watch for any unexpected symptoms. A rash, diarrhoea, a runny nose or more wind or crying than usual might suggest a food allergy or other sensitivity to that food. Discuss the next step with your baby's doctor or other professional health adviser.

FOODS MOST LIKELY TO CAUSE ALLERGIES

Peanuts and other nuts Peanuts can cause anaphylactic shock, a particularly severe allergic reaction where the throat swells and breathing gets difficult. Those who are prone must take great care to avoid peanuts, peanut butter and unrefined peanut oil, particularly in ready meals and snacks. Always read food labels carefully.

Seek advice from a health professional if you have a family history of peanut allergy, hay fever, asthma or eczema and if so, do not offer peanuts in any form to a child under three years old and then only under close supervision. It is rare to be allergic to other nuts, such as hazelnuts, walnuts or almonds, but seek advice from your doctor before introducing these.

Offer a child without a history of food allergy very finely ground almonds or hazelnuts at nine to 12 months and ground peanuts from 12 months. Do not give whole nuts to children under five years old.

Dairy products Some children lack lactase – the enzyme needed to digest milk sugar. Tummy aches and diarrhoea are possible indications, so consult your doctor if worried. Affected children may need to limit or omit cow's milk, cheese and butter from their diet. Soya milk and other soya products are suitable substitutes. Yogurt may be tolerated. Some babies may also be allergic to cow's milk protein (and soya-based milks too) and will require a hypoallergenic milk formula available on prescription from the doctor.

Gluten Gluten is a protein found in wheat, barley, rye and sometimes oats, as well as wheat-based products, such as bread and pasta. In some susceptible infants, eating it can lead to the development of coeliac disease whereby the small intestine is damaged. This impairs the absorption of nutrients, causing weight loss. This is highly unlikely to happen, but it is safer to reduce the risks. If this intolerance runs in the family, the mother will be advised to breastfeed exclusively for up to six months, preferably longer, and to delay introducing gluten-containing foods until the baby is at least nine months old (and wheat until the baby is over 12 months).

Babies with gluten intolerance may suffer from damage to the intestine lining, causing diarrhoea and other tummy problems, and weight loss. If diagnosed, choose rice cakes instead of bread, rice or corn noodles instead of wheat pasta, and buy rice or corn (maize) cereals for breakfast. You can also use buckwheat, millet and sorghum.

Eggs These can cause problems in a number of children. Rashes, swelling and tummy upsets are possible indicators.

Tomatoes These can cause eczema in young children. If your family has a history of allergies, don't include tomatoes in your child's diet until she is at least nine months old. Tomatoes may also be associated with hyperactivity.

Citrus fruit and strawberries A reaction to these may bring your baby out in a rash. If she is allergic, don't re-introduce these fruits until your baby is over 12 months.

Additives Hyperactivity in children is often attributed to certain artificial colourings, flavourings and sweeteners. Read food labels carefully.

food safety

Only give your baby or toddler food that looks and smells good. Throw it away if it's at all doubtful – at best it won't taste nice. At worst it could cause gastroenteritis or food poisoning.

PREPARING FRUIT AND VEGETABLES
Wash vegetables and fruit before eating them raw or cooking them unpeeled, to remove dirt and pesticide residues. Peel carrots and other root vegetables unless they're organic. If you want to grate the rind or liquidize whole citrus fruit, buy unwaxed fruit. Wash and peel vegetables and fruit immediately before serving; otherwise enzymes will react with the air to turn the cut surface brown, and they'll lose vitamin C.

REHEATING IN A MICROWAVE
A microwave oven heats food differently from a conventional oven, with heat spreading from the outside edges towards the centre. To compensate for this, always

food storage: do's and don'ts

DO

✔ Refrigerate or freeze meat, poultry, fish and dairy products

✔ Defrost frozen meat, poultry and fish in the refrigerator

✔ Keep raw meat, poultry and fish separate from other foods, and never allow their juices to drip on to other food

✔ Keep dried foods in sealed containers, and frozen food in airtight containers

✔ Cook meat and poultry thoroughly, until the juices run clear when you test the meatiest part with a knife

✔ Refrigerate leftovers at once and keep for 1–2 days, or throw them away.

DON'T

✘ Never give your family food past its 'use-by' date

✘ Don't let the fridge temperature rise above 4°C (40°F), or the freezer temperature above -18°C (0°F)

✘ Don't leave foods in the freezer too long. Use them in rotation, and check how long each food can safely be frozen for

✘ Don't use the same chopping board for cutting raw meat and other foods. After preparing raw meat and fish, wash your hands, knife and chopping board thoroughly before touching other foods, or your baby.

stir foods well. Allow a few minutes for food to stand and for heat to equalize throughout, then stir again and check the temperature before serving.

The other temptation is to heat foods until just lukewarm, but this will cause any bacteria present to multiply. Make sure food is piping hot first and then leave to cool to the correct serving temperature. Stir again and always check the temperature before serving.

Reheating foods more than once provides ideal conditions for bacteria to multiply and for food poisoning to follow, so always throw leftovers away.

don't forget

- Always cover just-cooked food and transfer to the refrigerator as soon as possible

- Never reheat food more than once

- Make sure reheated foods are piping hot, stir well and then leave to cool to the desired temperature

- If using a microwave, leave foods to stand after cooking and always stir well to prevent hotspots

6 laws of hygiene

1 Wash your hands thoroughly before preparing milk feeds and baby food.

2 Wash chopping boards, utensils and saucepans thoroughly in a dishwasher, or hand-wash in hot soapy water and rinse with boiling water.

3 Sterilize smaller items in a steam sterilizer, a saucepan of boiling water for five minutes, or in a cold water solution with sterilizing fluid or tablets, making sure items in water are completely immersed.

4 Sterilize bottles, caps, teats and bottle brushes each time you use them, whatever your child's age. There's no need to sterilize spoons, bowls, plates and cups used when feeding babies with solids, as long as you wash them thoroughly.

5 Keep kitchen worktops scrupulously clean and never allow pets to climb on them.

6 Change tea towels and cloths or sponges frequently.

the food pyramid

Providing a balanced diet is easy with the help of the food pyramid. All you need to do is give the different food groups in the proportions shown; choose a variety of foods from each layer; and follow the suggested number and size of helpings.

the different layers of the pyramid

1

FATS AND SUGAR

2

PROTEIN-RICH FOODS

3

VEGETABLES AND FRUIT

4

GRAINS, CEREALS AND BREAD

The pyramid shows the proportion of food from each group (grains; vegetables and fruits; proteins; fats and added sugar) to offer your family and eat yourself each day. Each layer represents a group of foods.

To create a well-balanced main meal, imagine the food on the plate. The largest amount should be the grains; the smallest should be the added sugars, and concentrated fats such as butter and oil.

using the food pyramid

1 fats and sugar

These include vegetable oils, butter, cream cheese, cream, mayonnaise, sugar, cakes, biscuits, sweets, honey, jam, maple syrup, ice cream and soft drinks.

Aim to minimize fatty and sugary foods. Children need fats, but they are present in many other valuable foods, including milk, cheese, yogurt, meat, chicken, oily fish, eggs, nuts and seeds. Neither children nor adults should have much in the way of concentrated fats from the first layer.

NB: The following guide to the food pyramid layers includes indications of portion size. Note that the cup used for some portion measures has a 250 ml (8 fl oz) capacity.

2 protein-rich foods

These include dairy foods like milk, cheese, fromage frais and yogurt; other animal protein foods like meat, poultry, game, fish and eggs; and vegetable protein like beans, tofu, peas and lentils.

A STANDARD CHILD HELPING IS:

- 50–75 g (2–3 oz) of meat, fish or cheese
- 2 medium eggs
- ½ cup cooked beans or lentils

3 vegetables and fruit

Offer children a variety of vegetables including starchy ones, like potatoes, carrots and swede; green leafy vegetables, such as cabbage, broccoli and spinach; and yellow-orange vegetables, such as carrots, pumpkin, sweet potato and squash.

Give children plenty of different fruits, too, including citrus fruits, like oranges and grapefruit; yellow-orange fruits, such as mangoes and apricots; berry fruits; and tree fruits, like apples, pears and plums.

A STANDARD CHILD HELPING IS:

- 1 cup of raw leafy vegetable, like lettuce or spinach
- ½ cup of other raw vegetables, or cooked vegetables
- 1 medium apple, pear or orange
- 1 melon wedge or slice of pineapple
- ½ grapefruit, mango or papaya
- ½ cup of fresh grapes or berries
- ½ cup of canned or stewed fruit
- ¼ cup of dried fruit
- 175 ml (6 fl oz) vegetable or fruit juice

4 grains, cereals and bread

These include wheat, barley, oats, corn and rice. Wholemeal and wholewheat grains and bread are better for your child than refined, white pasta, bread, rice etc.

A STANDARD CHILD HELPING IS:

- 1 slice of bread
- ½ cup of cooked pasta
- ½ cup of cooked porridge
- 25 g (1 oz) breakfast cereal
- ½ cup of cooked rice

meal planning

Use the Food Pyramid (see page 26) as a guide to planning your family's meals, but remember the number of daily helpings from each food group are guidelines only rather than set rules.

Appetites can vary a lot from day to day, so don't worry if your child doesn't always eat the suggested number of portions a day, or sometimes wants only very small helpings. It's the overall balance over the week that's more important.

MEAL PLANNING
for 1–6 months

Young babies should obtain all their nourishment from breast (or formula) milk. A baby in this age range who is hungry probably needs more milk, rather than solids. If you're breastfeeding and your baby is hungry, boost your milk supply to meet his needs simply by feeding more often, and for longer at each feed. Do this for two or three days and you should have plenty again. If your baby is extra hungry it may indicate he or she is going through a 'growth spurt'.

Some babies may start weaning at four months (see page 10).

MEAL PLANNING
for 6–9 months

If you are introducing solids for the first time, follow the guidelines on pages 10–12. If your baby is already taking solids, gradually increase the frequency over the weeks and months to three mini-meals daily, spaced as evenly as possible throughout the day. Build on the flavours your baby already enjoys and introduce simple combinations with new flavours too.

Be guided by your baby's preferences and don't hurry him. Too many flavours in quick succession may completely put him off the idea of solids. Aim to increase his solid foods gradually and maintain regular milk feeds.

Greater variety

Once your baby is happily eating different vegetables, try introducing ones with a slightly stronger flavour, such as parsnips, leeks and sweet pepper, but use small quantities to begin with and mix them with familiar, blander vegetables.

FINGER FOODS

Give an older baby 'finger foods' – foods to hold and suck on or chew. Many six-months-olds like to try holding food, and by eight or nine months they can cope very well. Try a large wedge of peeled raw fruit, such as an apple or rusks made from baked slices of wholemeal bread.

You can offer your baby a wider variety of fruit, including raw avocado, papaya, banana and melon. Offer new fruits one at a time until you know your baby likes them. You can then try combining fruits – perhaps a little cooked apple with some banana, or melon with pear. Papaya may sound a little exotic for a baby, but once it has been peeled and the seeds removed, it blends to a wonderfully smooth, vibrant orange purée. As it contains the enzyme papain, it is also very easy for a baby to digest.

While many vegetables no longer need sieving, fruits with skins, such as apricots and plums, need cooking and sieving. For a baby who doesn't seem keen on fruit, mix equal quantities of fruit purée and baby rice for a milder, milkier flavour.

Nutrients

Your baby's natural store of iron will now be exhausted, so it's important to include sufficient iron in the diet. A baby's appetite is small and his growth rate high, so it's also vital to provide foods that are a concentrated source of nutrients. Meals may now be thicker smooth purées, moving on to finely mashed or minced meals when your baby is ready.

PORTIONS

Once your baby is having solids three times a day aim to include:

- **2–3 mini-helpings** of starchy carbohydrate foods, such as potatoes or rice

- **2 mini-helpings** of fruit and vegetables (including potatoes, beans or peas if not counted as a starchy alternative to grains)

- **1 mini-helping** of a protein-rich food, such as cheese, meat or egg

ALLERGIES

If you have a family history of food allergies or related allergies, such as asthma or eczema, you may be advised to avoid giving your baby dairy products and eggs until much later. Avoid nuts until a child is three years. See also food allergies on pages 22–23.

FOODS TO AVOID

Nuts, oily fish, shellfish, salt, sugar, honey and offal.

MEAL PLANNING
for 9–12 months-olds

By now, your baby may be happy to progress to slightly lumpier food, especially if she has a few milk teeth, but be guided by her. Some babies hate lumps of any kind, while others are ready to try lots of new tastes and textures. The most important thing at this stage is to offer variety. If the diet is very limited now, then it can be difficult to encourage children to try novel foods later on.

New foods to try
Small portions of well-cooked and mashed frozen peas, dried split peas and chickpeas may now be offered. Provided that an allergy is not a consideration (see pages 22–23), smooth nut and seed butters can be introduced; simply grind lightly toasted hazelnuts, almonds, sunflower or sesame seeds, then blend to a paste with a little vegetable or sunflower oil.

Your child's repertoire of fish and meat can be extended by offering small amounts of oily fish, but always be extremely vigilant about checking for any bones. However, fish canned in brine should be avoided as it is too salty to be safe for a small child. If using small quantities of pulses, you may prefer to use canned beans for convenience; choose a variety without added salt or sugar. Canned tomatoes are also a good store-cupboard ingredient, but use them sparingly as they can be too acidic for young children. Whole eggs may now be used, but make sure they are cooked until both the yolk and white are firm.

If you and your family eat a balanced diet and feed your child what you all eat, you won't go far wrong, as long as you cut out added salt and use very little added sugar.

PORTIONS
A 9–12 month baby can be offered the following each day:

- **3–4 helpings** of starchy carbohydrate foods

- **3–4 helpings** of fruit and vegetables (including potatoes, beans or peas if not counted as a starchy alternative to grains)

- **1–2 helpings** of a protein-rich food, such as meat, fish, eggs or cheese

FOODS TO AVOID
Blue and unpasteurized cheeses, salt, sugar, honey, peanuts and shellfish.

the importance of snacks

Once your child is on the move, she can be incredibly active. While her energy and protein requirements are high in relation to her size, her appetite may be very small and it can be difficult to meet these dietary needs from just three main meals a day. Healthy but small snacks – those not laden with sugar or salt – can make all the difference. Choose from the following suggestions:

- Plain fromage frais with a little chopped fruit stirred in by you

- Diced mild Cheddar cheese

- A few bread sticks

- Half a rice cake

- Mini sandwiches made with cream cheese and banana, finely grated carrot and cheese

- Toast fingers

- Mini hot cross bun, cut into strips

- Carrot or cucumber sticks

- Half a banana

chopped banana and apple

fromage frais

carrot or cucumber sticks

half a rice cake

MEAL PLANNING
for 1–3 years

When your baby is one year old, milk will probably still be providing at least half of the calories and nourishment needed each day, and perhaps much more, because not all one-year-olds are eager to eat much in the way of solids.

From now on, the solids you give at breakfast, lunch and tea can gradually begin to take over from milk as the main source of nourishment, though milk will continue to be an important food for several years in most children.

If you are breastfeeding, you can give some full-fat cow's milk as well if you like. If you are bottle-feeding, you can give your baby full-fat cow's milk instead of formula milk now. Cow's milk is fairly low in iron, so if your child is bottle-fed and slow to take to solids, favour iron-rich foods and ask the doctor whether an iron supplement would be a good idea. Breast milk is richer in iron, so iron-deficiency anaemia is unlikely to occur in breastfed one-year-olds who don't yet eat many solids.

MAIN MEALS

Breakfast, lunch and supper are the main meals of the day, though many over-ones prefer to eat five or more smaller meals each day. This is easy if you give a snack mid-morning and at teatime, and perhaps a bedtime snack too (see box, page 31). One advantage of 'grazing' is that a child doesn't get irritable through hunger between meals. 'Grazing' also works for a child who is 'put-off' by large meals.

Make sure you give your child enough foods containing calcium, iron and vitamins, and avoid too many foods that contain added salt and sugar.

Breakfast

Most nutritionists regard breakfast as the most important meal of the day as it provides fuel and nutrients for the whole body, including the brain. A well-balanced, filling breakfast keeps a child going and, perhaps with a small top-up from a mid-morning snack, prevents a late-morning energy slump.

Lunch

This should be well balanced, and quite substantial, as it may have to provide nutrients and energy to last for some hours.

PORTIONS

A 1–3-year-old can be offered the following each day:

- **3–4 helpings** of starchy carbohydrate foods

- **3–4 helpings** of fruit and vegetables (including potatoes, beans or peas if not counted as a starchy alternative to grains)

- **1 helping** of a non-dairy protein-rich food

- **2–3 helpings** of full-fat milk or other dairy produce. Depending on how much other fat your child consumes, you may wish to introduce semi-skimmed milk when they reach the age of two.

FOODS TO AVOID
Nuts

Supper

This meal can be smaller than the other main meals. Some children sleep better after a supper that's rich in carbohydrate, but not so rich in protein. Any sort of pasta dish is an excellent choice.

Snacks

Try to make these 'mini meals' nutritious. Avoid sugary cakes and biscuits or fatty, salty crisps. Instead, offer fresh or dried fruit, or perhaps vegetable sticks with a dip, a small sandwich or a smoothie.

FOOD CONCERNS

Be relaxed about your child's food intake, because he or she will readily pick up any anxiety on your part.

As your baby grows into a toddler, try to offer the same balanced diet as the rest of the family eats. Toddlers shouldn't live on 'nursery food' – bland, smooth, 'white' foods – though like kids of all ages, they may enjoy them from time to time.

Young children usually eat better if they are in company, where the attention isn't focused solely on what and how much they eat. So aim for you and your toddler – or the whole family – to eat together whenever possible, and use the time for listening to and learning about each other.

MEAL PLANNING
for over 3 years

Trust your child to eat what he or she needs. There's every reason to suppose this will happen, provided you don't offer too much food laden with sugar and fat. Never force a child to eat, but don't compensate half an hour afterwards by offering a 'junk-food' snack, high in calories, sugar and/or fat, but with relatively few other nutrients, or the lesson will be that refusing a meal means he or she can then have 'junk food'. Give a healthy snack (see page 21) instead. There's nothing wrong with junk food occasionally, but too much on a regular basis can lead to bad moods and behaviour problems, being overweight and nutritional deficiencies.

School children

A good breakfast helps a child to stay full of energy, and learn well. Choosing what to give your child to take to school for a mid-morning snack can be a challenge because children often want what others are eating. So if this happens to be 'junk' food, they'll probably want a chocolate bar, rather than something more nutritious. For a young child, try making your healthy 'break' look attractive – perhaps by wrapping it up in shiny cellophane.

Many schoolchildren are very active and need the sort of food and drink that will help keep them full of energy. So for breakfast, break and lunch, include some foods that supply a steady source of slow-release energy, such as bananas, Oat and Apple Muffins (see page 120) or Carrot Cakes (see page 123).

PORTIONS

Each day, aim to offer:

- **6–11 helpings** of starchy carbohydrate foods – this sounds a lot, but six helpings soon adds up, or you can make up the balance by offering starchy choices from other layers of the pyramid, such as potatoes, carrots or bananas

- **5 helpings** of fruit and vegetables (including potatoes, beans or peas if not counted as a starchy alternative to grains)

- **2–3 helpings** of protein-rich foods.

Also, each week, include:

- **2–3 helpings** of beans, bean products, or peas (counted either as starchy alternatives to grains, or as vegetables)

- **2–3 helpings** of oily fish (counted as protein)

- **No more than 3 helpings** of beef, lamb or pork, as these red meats contain a relatively high proportion of saturated fats.

vegetarian and vegan children

If your child is vegetarian, offer plenty of foods containing iron and vitamin B12, as these are the nutrients most likely to be lacking. Also, offer any two of the following three food groups each day:

- **Milk** – fresh milk, cheese or yogurt
- **Bread** – bread, cereals, other grain foods; or actual grains
- **Beans** – beans, peas or lentils

If your child is a vegan, check with your doctor that her diet is nutritionally adequate and discuss whether there is a need for any supplement – for example, of vitamin B12. Zen macrobiotic and fruitarian diets are unsuitable for young children.

a healthy body weight

It's normal for many young children to be a little plump. A few, though, are too plump. And a few are too thin. If necessary a doctor can plot your child's weight on a chart. If the weight is very high or low – or if it's quickly heading that way – you should be concerned.

Children naturally tend to become more streamlined as they approach five years. However, older children are more likely to be heavy if they have overweight parents. So if your child has a weight problem and you do too, do something about yourself before focusing on them. Your example of healthy eating and exercising may do more to help your overweight child than anything else.

babies

The recipes in this section offer a changing menu of tastes and textures for young babies experiencing their first foods. If you are starting weaning at four months, simply follow the recipes for six months and progress gradually.

adapting recipes

Some of the recipes give suggestions for adapting them for toddlers, as the smooth purées discourage chewing.

replacing formula milk with breast milk

If you prefer to use breast milk rather than formula milk in the purée recipes, add just before serving, remembering to estimate the amount of milk needed per individual portion.

recipe contents

butternut squash purée

Butternut squash makes the most wonderful, vibrant, fine orange purée and is an ideal vegetable to freeze.

3 SERVINGS

250 g (8 oz) butternut squash, peeled, deseeded and diced

6 tablespoons formula milk (or breast milk – see box, page 36)

1 Rinse the butternut squash with boiled water and drain. Place the squash in a steamer, cover and steam for 10 minutes until tender. Transfer to a blender and purée, gradually adding the milk until smooth. Sieve if necessary.

2 Spoon one portion into a bowl and serve. Cover and chill the remainder, then freeze in sections of an ice cube tray.

✳ TIPS

For a bright green alternative, cook and purée diced courgette in the same way. Sieve the purée for young babies.

The larger the dice, the longer they will take to cook.

root vegetable harvest

Root vegetables, such as parsnips, carrots and swedes, are ideal weaning foods as babies love their natural sweetness.

4 SERVINGS

175 g (6 oz) parsnip, peeled and diced

125 g (4 oz) carrot, peeled and diced

200–250 ml (7–8 fl oz) formula milk or boiled water (or breast milk – see box, page 36)

1 Rinse the vegetables with boiled water and put into a small saucepan with 150 ml (¼ pint) of the milk or water. Cover and simmer for 15 minutes or until the vegetables are very tender. Place in a blender and purée with the remaining milk or water until smooth, then press through a sieve.

2 Spoon one portion into a bowl and serve. Cover and chill the remainder, then freeze in sections of an ice cube tray.

✳ TIP
You could use swede, potato or sweet potato if you prefer.

broccoli and potato purée

This mild first taste of green vegetables is a good source of folic acid and vitamin C. Serve at lunchtime as broccoli can make a baby windy.

2–3 SERVINGS

125 g (4 oz) potato, peeled and diced

200–250 ml (7–8 fl oz) formula milk or boiled water (or breast milk – see box, page 36)

75 g (3 oz) broccoli, cut into small florets, stems sliced

1 Rinse the potato with boiled water, drain and put into a small saucepan with 150 ml (¼ pint) of the milk or water. Cover and simmer for 10 minutes. Add the broccoli, cover and cook for 5 more minutes, until the vegetables are just tender. Place in a blender and purée, gradually adding the remaining milk or water, then press through a sieve if required.

2 Spoon one portion into a bowl and serve. Cover and chill the remainder, then freeze in sections of an ice cube tray.

✱ TIP
As weaning becomes more established, you will be able to stop sieving foods, but do make sure purées are still smooth at this stage.

squash and lentil bake

The sweet taste of the butternut, combined with the mineral-rich lentils, make this a nutrient-packed starter food.

4–5 SERVINGS

125 g (4 oz) butternut squash, peeled, deseeded and diced

25 g (1 oz) red lentils, well washed

175–200 ml (6–7 fl oz) boiled water

1 teaspoon vegetable oil

1 Rinse the butternut squash with boiled water and put into a small saucepan with the lentils and 150 ml (¼ pint) of the water. Cover and simmer for 30 minutes until the lentils are very soft. Place in a blender with the remaining water and the oil and purée until smooth, then press through a sieve.

2 Spoon one portion into a bowl and serve. Cover and chill the remainder, then freeze in sections of an ice cube tray.

✳ TIP
If using a microwave to reheat baby food, stir the food thoroughly to disperse any hot spots and always test the temperature of your baby's food before serving.

chicken chowder

Packed with protein, this creamy smooth purée has just a hint of chicken flavour. The carrot gives an appealing orange colour.

2–3 SERVINGS

125 g (4 oz) potato, peeled and diced

50 g (2 oz) carrot, peeled and diced

50 g (2 oz) skinless, boneless chicken breast, diced

150–200 ml (5–7 fl oz) formula milk or boiled water (or breast milk – see box, page 36)

1 Rinse the potato, carrot and chicken with boiled water. Drain and put into a small saucepan with 150 ml (¼ pint) of the milk or water. Cover and simmer for 15 minutes, until the vegetables are tender and the chicken is thoroughly cooked. Place in a blender and purée, gradually adding the remaining milk or water, if necessary, until smooth, then press through a sieve.

2 Spoon one portion into a bowl and serve. Cover and chill the remainder, then freeze in sections of an ice cube tray.

✳ TIP
If the chicken is simmered over a very low heat, you will probably not need to add the extra milk or water when puréeing.

sweet potato and apple purée

Don't be afraid of mixing fruit with vegetables – many combinations, such as this one, work extremely well.

4–5 SERVINGS

1 sweet potato, about 200 g (7 oz), peeled and diced

1 dessert apple, peeled, cored and diced

175–200 ml (6–7 fl oz) formula milk or boiled water (or breast milk – see box, page 36)

1 Rinse the sweet potato with boiled water and put into a small saucepan with the apple and 150 ml (¼ pint) of the milk or water. Cover and simmer for 12–15 minutes until the sweet potato is tender.

2 Place the mixture in a blender with the remaining milk or water and purée until smooth, then press through a sieve.

3 Spoon one portion into a bowl and serve. Cover and chill the remainder, then freeze in sections of an ice cube tray.

✳ TIP
Try combining apple with carrot or parsnip to make a deliciously sweet purée.

apple and pear duet

Make sure that you choose sweet and ripe fruit, or your baby may be put off by the tartness of this pudding.

3–4 SERVINGS

1 dessert apple, peeled, cored and diced

1 ripe pear, peeled, cored and diced

3 tablespoons boiled water

1 Put all the ingredients into a small saucepan, cover and simmer for 10 minutes until very soft, then press through a sieve.

2 Spoon one portion into a bowl and serve. Cover and chill the remainder, then freeze in sections of an ice cube tray.

∗ TIP
Once you know that your baby likes apple and pear, you can try adding other fruits to this duet – for example apricots, peaches or nectarines.

apricot and millet fool

This delicious fool is adored by most babies. If you can't buy fresh apricots, then use ripe, sweet-tasting plums or fresh peaches instead.

2–3 SERVINGS

2 tablespoons millet flakes

3 small apricots, well washed, pitted and diced

200 ml (7 fl oz) formula milk or boiled water (or breast milk – see box, page 36)

1 Put all the ingredients into a small saucepan and bring to the boil over a low heat. Cook, stirring constantly, for 4–5 minutes, until thickened and the apricots are soft. Process in a blender, then press through a sieve to remove the apricot skins.

2 Spoon one portion into a bowl and serve. Cover and chill the remainder, then freeze in sections of an ice cube tray.

✳ TIP
As the mixture thickens on cooling, you may need to thin it with a little extra milk or water before serving.

carrot and red pepper ambrosia

Quick and easy to make, this brightly coloured purée is bound to attract your baby's attention.

2 SERVINGS

1 carrot, about 125 g (4 oz), peeled and diced

¼ red pepper, cored, deseeded and diced

25 g (1 oz) risotto rice, rinsed

200 ml (7 fl oz) homemade vegetable stock (see page 126) or water

1 fresh rosemary sprig (optional)

2–3 tablespoons full-fat milk

1 Put the carrot, red pepper, rice and stock or water into a saucepan. Add the rosemary, if using. Bring to the boil, partially cover the pan and simmer for 15 minutes, or until the rice is tender and most of the liquid is absorbed. Discard the rosemary.

2 Place the vegetables and rice in a blender and process, adding enough milk to make a smooth thick purée, adjusting the texture as your baby matures.

3 Serve half straight away, then cover and chill the rest and use within 24 hours, or freeze for another meal. Add a little extra water or milk before serving if needed.

FOR OLDER BABIES AND TODDLERS
Adjust the consistency to a coarser purée as your baby matures, moving on to a mashed or chopped texture as your baby approaches his first birthday.

For toddlers, there is no need to purée the mixture. Serve accompanied by warmed bread for extra texture.

✳ TIPS
As the rice grains swell on standing, you may need to add a little extra water or milk to loosen the consistency before serving.

If you haven't any risotto rice, use long-grain white rice instead. Alternatively, substitute quinoa, adjusting the cooking time and topping up with extra stock or water as needed.

creamy vegetable pasta

Here, broccoli and green beans boost nutrient levels, and cream cheese melts to make a delicious sauce for small pasta shapes.

2 SERVINGS

40 g (1½ oz) tagliatelle, macaroni or small pasta shapes

50 g (2 oz) broccoli, cut into small florets, stems sliced

25 g (1 oz) green beans, sliced

3 tablespoons full-fat cream cheese

few fresh basil leaves (optional)

3–5 tablespoons full-fat milk

1 Cook the pasta in a saucepan of boiling water for 6–8 minutes or until tender. Meanwhile, steam the broccoli florets and green beans for 5 minutes until tender.

2 Drain the cooked pasta and place in a blender with the vegetables, cream cheese and basil, if using. Blend, adding enough milk to make a smooth purée.

3 Serve half straight away, then cover and chill the rest and use within 24 hours, or freeze for another meal. Add a little extra water or milk before serving if needed.

FOR OLDER BABIES AND TODDLERS
Finely chop rather than purée the mixture for older babies, and flavour with a little garlic and extra freshly chopped herbs.

You can use ready flavoured garlic and herb cream cheese for cver-ones.

✳ TIP
Like rice, pasta swells as it stands so you may need to stir a little extra milk into the second pasta meal before serving to your baby.

baby spinach dhal

This mildly spiced dhal suits very young tastebuds and the red lentils are a good way to introduce a little fibre into your baby's diet.

2 SERVINGS

40 g (1½ oz) red lentils, rinsed

25 g (1 oz) long-grain white rice

1 teaspoon vegetable oil

pinch of ground coriander

pinch of ground turmeric

250 ml (8 fl oz) homemade vegetable stock (see page 126) or water

25 g (1 oz) frozen chopped spinach, just defrosted, or fresh spinach (prepared weight)

1 fresh tomato, skinned, deseeded and finely chopped

1 Put the lentils, rice, oil, spices and stock or water into a saucepan and bring to the boil. Cover and simmer for 25 minutes or until the lentils are soft, stirring occasionally and topping up with extra water or stock if needed.

2 Stir in the spinach and chopped tomato and cook for 2 minutes. Place in a blender and process to a smooth thick purée, adjusting the texture as your baby matures.

3 Serve half straight away, then cover and chill the rest and use within 24 hours.

FOR OLDER BABIES AND TODDLERS

As your baby's tastes become more adventurous you may like to add a little finely crushed garlic or a little fried diced onion.

* TIP

Tomatoes can cause an allergic reaction in a few children, so watch your baby closely the first time you include them in the diet.

creamed parsnip and tofu

Blended with mashed parsnip, tofu takes on a mild creaminess and makes a simple supper that is packed with protein.

2 SERVINGS

2 small parsnips, about 300 g (10 oz), peeled and diced

50 g (2 oz) tofu, drained and crumbled

1 tablespoon fresh orange juice

100–150 ml (3½–5 fl oz) full-fat milk

1 Place the parsnips in a steamer, cover, and cook for 10 minutes until just soft.

2 Put the parsnips in a blender and add the tofu and orange juice. Blend until smooth, gradually adding enough milk to make a smooth thick purée.

3 Serve half straight away, then cover and chill the rest and use within 24 hours, or freeze for another meal. Add a little extra water or milk before serving if needed.

FOR OLDER BABIES AND TODDLERS
Mash the parsnips and tofu more coarsely and increase the orange juice slightly for a stronger flavour. Serve with finger foods or stir-fried mixed vegetables for extra crunch.

✻ TIPS
If your baby seems to have lost his appetite, then this is a good choice to tempt him with as the purée is slightly sweet.

Adjust the thickness of the purée as your baby matures.

Give your baby small amounts of tofu early on – he is more likely to be receptive now than if he first tastes it as an older child.

cock-a-leekie stew

As your baby grows and enjoys solid foods, you can begin to include foods with a little more flavour, such as dried or fresh herbs.

3 SERVINGS

200 g (7 oz) potato, peeled and diced

125 g (4 oz) skinless, boneless chicken breast, diced

75 g (3 oz) carrot, peeled and diced

2.5 cm (1 inch) piece leek, rinsed, halved and thinly sliced

1 ready-to-eat pitted prune, quartered

pinch mixed dried herbs

200 ml (7 fl oz) boiled water

FOR OLDER BABIES AND TODDLERS

As your baby grows and has more teeth, adjust the texture from a smooth, thick purée to a mashed, and, later, a finely chopped mixture.

Encourage your child to take an active part in the meal by offering a second spoon for him to play with.

1 Put the potato, chicken and carrot into a small saucepan with the leek, prune and herbs. Pour in the water, bring to the boil, then cover and simmer gently for 20 minutes.

2 Spoon the vegetables, chicken, prune and half the cooking liquid into a blender and process to the desired texture, gradually adding the remaining liquid if required.

3 Serve one portion straight away, then cover and chill the rest and use within 24 hours, or freeze in individual portions for another meal. Add a little extra water or milk if needed.

✳ TIP
Homemade, salt-free chicken stock may be added instead of water. Do not use stock cubes.

51

plaice florentine

Plaice has such a delicate flavour that it's sure to win round even the most reluctant of fish eaters.

3 SERVINGS

1 small fillet of plaice, rinsed

200 g (7 oz) potato, peeled and diced

200 ml (7 fl oz) full-fat milk

125 g (4 oz) courgette, trimmed and diced

3 watercress sprigs

1 tablespoon mascarpone cheese

✳ TIPS

The mascarpone adds a wonderful creaminess to the sauce, but you could use full-fat cream cheese, ricotta, cottage or grated Cheddar cheese instead.

Pink trout fillets are also delicious. As with all fish, check carefully for bones and sieve the fish to make sure.

FOR OLDER BABIES AND TODDLERS
Blend only briefly, so that your child starts to eat chunks of fish and vegetables.

1 Cook the fish, covered, in a steamer for 5 minutes, or until the fish is opaque and flakes easily. Alternatively, poach in a shallow pan containing a 1 cm (½ inch) depth of simmering water until just tender. Flake the fish, carefully removing any bones.

2 Meanwhile, simmer the potato and milk in a covered small saucepan for 5 minutes. Add the courgette and cook for 3 minutes. Add the watercress and cook for 2 more minutes. Drain, reserving the milk.

3 Put the fish into a blender with the vegetables, mascarpone and half the milk. Process to the desired texture, gradually adding the milk as needed.

4 Serve one portion straight away, then cover and chill the rest and use within 24 hours, or freeze in individual portions for another meal.

baby cauliflower cheese

You don't need to prepare a cheese sauce, simply purée all the ingredients together for a deliciously mild, quick-to-make, cheesy supper.

2 SERVINGS

150 g (5 oz) potato, peeled and diced

150 g (5 oz) cauliflower, cut into small florets

2.5 cm (1 inch) piece leek, rinsed and thinly sliced

40 g (1½ oz) mild Cheddar cheese, grated

75–125 ml (3–4 fl oz) full-fat milk

1 Put the potato in a steamer, cover, and cook for 10 minutes. Add the cauliflower and leek and cook for a further 5 minutes, until all the vegetables are just tender.

2 Transfer the steamed vegetables to a blender, add the cheese, and process, gradually adding enough milk to make a smooth, thick purée.

3 Serve half straight away, then cover and chill the rest and use within 24 hours, or freeze for another meal. Add a little extra water or milk before serving if needed.

FOR OLDER BABIES AND TODDLERS
Use less milk and mash the ingredients together rather than blending them to make a chunkier cauliflower cheese.

✳ TIP
Adding milk and cheese to baby meals is a good way to include plenty of protein and calcium in the diet, especially if your baby doesn't seem to be drinking as much milk. A 40 g (1½ oz) portion of Cheddar cheese is equivalent to 200 ml (7 fl oz) of milk.

pumpkin pilaf

For this baby pilaf, millet grains take the place of the more traditional rice. They are cooked with pumpkin and lightly flavoured with allspice.

2 SERVINGS

40 g (1½ oz) millet grain, rinsed

125 g (4 oz) pumpkin or butternut squash, peeled, deseeded and diced

1 tablespoon raisins (optional)

pinch of ground allspice

1 small bay leaf

300 ml (½ pint) homemade vegetable stock (see page 126), or water

FOR OLDER BABIES AND TODDLERS

Add 2 tablespoons of ground almonds with the other ingredients (unless allergy is a consideration). Adjust the texture, making the pilaf slightly coarser. Serve with cooked broccoli florets and warmed strips of pitta bread as finger foods.

For toddlers, add a little finely chopped fried onion and mushrooms and don't blend the pilaf.

1 Put all the ingredients into a saucepan and bring to the boil. Cover and simmer for 20–25 minutes until the millet is soft, topping up with extra stock or water as needed.

2 Discard the bay leaf. Place the mixture in a blender and process to a smooth thick purée, adjusting the texture as your baby matures.

3 Serve half straight away, then cover and chill the rest and use within 24 hours, or freeze for another meal. Add a little extra water or milk before serving if needed.

> ✳ TIP
> Millet flakes can be used instead of grains – reduce the cooking time to just 5 minutes and stir the mixture frequently as it thickens.

plum and ricotta purée

Plums are puréed and mixed with creamy Italian ricotta cheese to create a nutritious and deliciously sweet dessert.

2–3 SERVINGS

2 large ripe plums, about 200 g (7 oz), washed, pitted and roughly chopped

1 tablespoon water

pinch of ground cinnamon (optional)

3 tablespoons ricotta cheese

1 Put the plums in a small saucepan with the water and the cinnamon, if using. Cover and cook gently for 5 minutes, until soft. Remove from the heat and leave to cool.

2 Spoon the plums and ricotta into a blender and process until smooth. Press through a sieve to remove the skins.

3 Serve half or a third straight away, then cover and chill the rest and use within 24 hours, or freeze in individual portions for another meal.

FOR OLDER BABIES AND TODDLERS
Don't process the plums, but remove their skins and leave in chunks for your baby or toddler to chew on.

✳ TIP
For optimum sweetness, make larger amounts when fresh plums are plentiful and ripe and freeze portions for future use.

peach and apple fool

This creamy, smooth fool combines two naturally sweet fruits, with just a hint of cardamom for a delicious dessert.

2 SERVINGS

1 peach, rinsed, halved, pitted and roughly chopped

1 dessert apple, rinsed, quartered, cored and roughly chopped

1 tablespoon water

2 cardamom pods, bruised (optional)

2 tablespoons natural bio yogurt

1 Put the peach and apple into a small saucepan with the water and the cardamom pods, if using. Cover and simmer gently for 5 minutes, until the fruit is tender. Remove the cardamom pods and discard.

2 Put the fruit into a blender and purée until smooth, then press through a sieve to remove the fruit skins and cardamom seeds. Cover and leave to cool, then mix the purée with the yogurt.

3 Serve half straight away, then cover and chill the rest and use within 24 hours, or freeze for another meal. Add a little extra water or milk before serving if needed.

* TIP
For optimum flavour, use ripe peaches and naturally sweet dessert apples.

FOR OLDER BABIES AND TODDLERS
Toddlers can enjoy this as a sauce spooned over sliced peaches.

mediterranean vegetables with quinoa

Quinoa is a South American alternative to rice or couscous and a superior source of vegetable protein. It is available from most healthfood shops.

2 SERVINGS

1 teaspoon vegetable oil

1 tablespoon finely chopped onion

½ red pepper, cored, deseeded and finely chopped

½ orange pepper, cored, deseeded and finely chopped

½ medium courgette, about 75 g (3 oz), finely chopped

½ garlic clove, finely crushed (optional)

25 g (1 oz) quinoa, rinsed

½ teaspoon tomato purée

300 ml (½ pint) homemade vegetable stock (see page 126) or water

1 tomato, skinned, deseeded and finely chopped

2 teaspoons finely chopped fresh oregano, marjoram or basil (optional)

1 Heat the oil in a medium saucepan, add the onion and fry for 4–5 minutes until lightly browned. Add the peppers, courgette and garlic, if using, and fry for 3 minutes.

2 Stir in the quinoa, tomato purée and stock or water. Bring to the boil, then lower the heat, cover the pan and simmer for 20 minutes, or until the quinoa grains are soft. Add the chopped tomato and chopped herbs, if using. Cook, uncovered, for 3 minutes.

3 Mash well and serve half straight away. Cover and chill the rest and use within 24 hours, or freeze for another meal.

FOR OLDER BABIES AND TODDLERS
Chop up the mixture rather than mashing it so that the vegetables are still chunky.

✳ TIP
Add the tomato at the end of the cooking time as it provides more vitamin C that way and helps to boost iron and calcium absorption.

mixed vegetable dip

Sunflower seed paste gives this vegetarian feast a protein boost. Vary the vegetable mix with red peppers, green beans, parsnips and courgettes.

2 SERVINGS

1 small potato, about 125 g (4 oz), peeled and diced

1 small carrot, about 125 g (4 oz), peeled and diced

125 g (4 oz) butternut squash, peeled, deseeded and diced

50 g (2 oz) broccoli, cut into small florets, stems sliced

4 teaspoons sunflower seeds

1 teaspoon vegetable oil

2–3 tablespoons full-fat milk

FOR OLDER BABIES AND TODDLERS
Give them finger food such as carrot or cucumber sticks or breadsticks (see page 69) and let them dip in the vegetables or breadsticks.

Add a little diced cucumber, chopped pineapple or cheese.

You could use fortified soya milk instead of full-fat cow's milk.

1 Put the potato, carrot and squash into a steamer. Cover and steam for 10 minutes. Add the broccoli, cover again and cook for a further 5 minutes.

2 Meanwhile, grind the sunflower seeds to a smooth paste with the oil and 1 tablespoon of the milk in a food processor spice mill attachment or a well-washed coffee grinder. Alternatively, pound the seeds using a pestle and mortar, gradually adding the oil and milk.

3 Mash or chop the vegetables, mixing in the sunflower seed paste and enough milk to give the required consistency. Adjust the texture as your baby matures.

4 Serve half straight away, then cover and chill the rest and use within 24 hours.

✳ TIP
If possible, buy organically grown vegetables for your family's meals.

lentil hotpot

Now that your baby is getting older, you can flavour plain lentils by adding onion fried in a little oil or even a small amount of garlic.

2 SERVINGS

1 teaspoon vegetable oil

2 tablespoons onion, finely chopped

1 carrot, about 125 g (4 oz), peeled and diced

1 small potato, about 150 g (5 oz), peeled and diced

½ garlic clove, crushed (optional)

40 g (1½ oz) red lentils, rinsed

200 ml (7 fl oz) homemade vegetable stock (see page 126) or water

2 tablespoons fresh orange juice

1 tablespoon finely chopped fresh chives

1 Heat the oil in a medium saucepan, add the onion and fry for 4–5 minutes until lightly browned. Add the carrot, potato and garlic, if using, then stir in the lentils and stock or water. Bring to the boil, cover and simmer for 25 minutes, topping up with a little extra stock or water if needed.

2 Stir the orange juice and chives into the lentil mixture, then mash or chop to suit your baby.

3 Serve half straight away, then cover and chill the rest and use within 24 hours or freeze for another meal.

FOR OLDER BABIES AND TODDLERS
Instead of mashing the hotpot, chop it up into small pieces so that your child gets used to lumps.

✱ TIP
Add other vegetables to the hotpot that your child may be reluctant to try, such as peppers or courgette.

cheesy polenta with courgettes

Serving soft polenta with a chunkier chopped vegetable sauce is a good halfway meal to encourage your baby towards foods with more texture.

1 SERVING

1 teaspoon vegetable oil

50 g (2 oz) courgette, rinsed and finely diced

1 mushroom, rinsed and finely chopped

1 tomato, skinned, deseeded and finely chopped

½ teaspoon tomato purée

150 ml (¼ pint) water

25 g (1 oz) quick-cook polenta

25 g (1 oz) mild Cheddar cheese, grated

1 Heat the oil in a small saucepan, add the courgette and mushroom and fry, stirring, for 2–3 minutes, until very lightly browned. Add the tomato, tomato purée and 3 tablespoons of water. Cover and cook for 5 minutes.

2 Bring the remaining water to the boil in another small saucepan. Sprinkle in the polenta in a steady stream, stirring constantly. Cook over a medium heat, stirring constantly, for 1–2 minutes, until thickened.

3 Stir in the cheese and spoon into a serving bowl. Mash the vegetable sauce, if required. Spoon the sauce on top of the polenta and cool slightly before serving.

FOR OLDER BABIES AND TODDLERS
Try adding cooked, diced fish or meat, such as salmon or chicken, to the vegetable sauce.

✳ TIP
Young children need fat as a concentrated form of energy, but choose sources that are also rich in other nutrients. Cheese is a good example as it is rich in protein, calcium and the fat-soluble vitamins A, D, E and K.

moroccan lamb

Lightly spiced with just the tiniest amount of cinnamon and garlic, this slow-cooked casserole is the ideal next step towards family meals.

4 SERVINGS

1 teaspoon vegetable oil

125 g (4 oz) lean lamb steak, rinsed, trimmed and diced

2 teaspoons finely chopped onion

75 g (3 oz) potato, peeled and diced

75 g (3 oz) carrot, peeled and diced

1 ready-to-eat dried apricot, chopped

1 tablespoon sultanas

pinch of ground cinnamon

½ bay leaf

500 ml (17 fl oz) boiling water

75 g (3 oz) couscous

> **✳ TIP**
> Lamb is a good choice to try when you first feed your child red meat.

> **FOR OLDER BABIES AND TODDLERS**
> Mash or finely chop the lamb so that your child gets used to a lumpier mixture.

1 Heat the oil in a small flameproof casserole dish. Add the lamb and onion, and fry, stirring frequently, for 3 minutes, until browned. Add the potato, carrot, apricot, sultanas, cinnamon and bay leaf, then pour in 300 ml (½ pint) of the boiling water. Bring back to the boil, cover and cook in a preheated oven at 180°C (350°F), Gas Mark 4 for 1 hour.

2 Remove and discard the bay leaf. Reserve the stock. Put in a blender and process the lamb to the desired texture, gradually adding a little of the reserved stock, as needed.

3 Put the couscous into a bowl and pour over the remaining boiling water. Leave to stand for 5 minutes, then fluff up with a fork and stir into the lamb.

4 Serve one portion straight away, then cover and chill the rest and use within 24 hours.

cheat's carrot cassoulet

Forget about long, slow cooking in the oven, this cassoulet – made with canned haricot beans, carrots and parsnips – is cooked on the hob.

2 SERVINGS

1 carrot, about 125 g (4 oz), peeled and diced

1 small parsnip, about 150 g (5 oz), peeled and diced

2.5 cm (1 inch) piece leek, rinsed and thinly sliced

50 g (2 oz) canned haricot beans (without salt or sugar), rinsed

few fresh herb sprigs, such as sage, rosemary and marjoram

150 ml (¼ pint) homemade vegetable stock (see page 126) or water

1 tomato, skinned, deseeded and finely chopped

1 Put the carrot, parsnip, leek, haricot beans and herb sprigs into a medium saucepan. Add the stock or water and bring to the boil, then cover the pan. Lower the heat and simmer for 15 minutes, until the vegetables are tender, topping up with extra stock if needed.

2 Add the tomato and cook for a further 2–3 minutes, until softened, then discard the herb sprigs. Mash or chop the cassoulet to suit your baby's taste.

3 Serve half immediately. Cover and chill the remainder and use within 24 hours or freeze for another meal.

FOR OLDER BABIES AND TODDLERS
Add cooked lamb or chicken to the cassoulet.

✳ TIP
Buy canned baked beans without added salt or sugar or use home-cooked dried beans instead.

tuna ragu

Encourage your baby to try slightly coarser textures by stirring tiny pasta shapes, which are soft and easy to chew, into a smooth sauce.

4–5 SERVINGS

1 teaspoon vegetable oil

¼ onion, finely chopped

¼ red pepper, about 50 g (2 oz), deseeded and finely chopped

1 celery stick, about 75 g (3 oz), trimmed and finely chopped

½ courgette, about 75 g (3 oz), trimmed and finely chopped

1 carrot, about 125 g (4 oz), peeled and finely chopped

2 canned tomatoes

150 ml (¼ pint) water

100 g (3½ oz) can tuna in water, drained

75 g (3 oz) baby pasta

✳ TIP
Use tuna canned in water, not brine, as the latter is far too salty for your baby.

FOR OLDER BABIES AND TODDLERS
Don't chop the pasta or use larger pasta for toddlers.

1 Heat the oil in a medium saucepan, add the onion and fry, stirring frequently, for 4–5 minutes, until pale golden. Add the red pepper, celery, courgette and carrot, cook for 1 minute, then stir in the tomatoes and water. Cover and simmer for 15 minutes, until tender.

2 Pour the mixture into a blender and process until smooth. Finely flake the fish, then stir it into the sauce.

3 Fill a second saucepan with water and bring to the boil. Add the pasta and cook for 5 minutes, until tender. Drain the pasta, chop if necessary, then stir it into the sauce.

4 Reheat one portion and serve immediately. Cover and chill the rest of the ragu and use within 24 hours, or freeze in individual portions for another meal.

broccoli and fennel risotto

This light, fresh-tasting meal with a hint of lemon is quick and easy to put together and is ideal for a busy parent.

2 SERVINGS

1 teaspoon vegetable oil

50 g (2 oz) piece of fennel bulb, rinsed and finely chopped

50 g (2 oz) risotto rice, rinsed

300–350 ml (10–12 fl oz) homemade vegetable stock (see page 126) or water

1 egg

75 g (3 oz) broccoli, rinsed and cut into tiny florets, stems chopped

1 tablespoon lemon juice

✳ TIP
A risotto base is a good way to introduce your baby to more interesting vegetables and new combinations.

FOR OLDER BABIES AND TODDLERS
Boost protein by adding finely chopped tofu or ground almonds (if allergies are not a consideration).

1 Heat the oil in a medium saucepan, add the fennel and fry for 2–3 minutes, until softened. Stir in the rice and cook for 1 minute. Add three-quarters of the stock or water and bring to the boil. Simmer gently, uncovered, for 10 minutes.

2 Meanwhile, place the egg in a pan of boiling water and cook for 8 minutes to hard-boil. Drain and immerse in cold water, then set aside.

3 Add the broccoli to the rice. Cook for 5 minutes, stirring more frequently. Stir in the lemon juice.

4 Spoon half of the risotto into a bowl. Mash or chop if required. Peel the egg and finely chop half of it. Sprinkle over the risotto and serve.

5 Wrap the remaining egg half in clingfilm and store in the refrigerator. Cover and chill the remaining risotto and use within 24 hours.

eggy bread fingers

A great store-cupboard standby and ideal for a quick late breakfast, lunch or tea. Slightly stale bread will soon soften once coated in the egg.

2 SERVINGS

1 egg

2 teaspoons full-fat milk

2 teaspoons vegetable oil

small knob of unsalted butter

2 slices bread, crusts removed, halved

1 Beat the egg and milk together in a shallow dish. Heat the oil and butter together in a large frying pan. Quickly dip each piece of bread into the egg mixture and turn to coat. Add to the pan and repeat with the second slice of bread.

2 Fry for 2–3 minutes, until golden, then turn over and cook the second side for 2–3 minutes. Remove the bread from the pan and cut into finger-size strips. Allow to cool slightly, then serve a few at time.

FOR OLDER BABIES AND TODDLERS
Keep a watchful eye on young children when they are eating, especially when they feed themselves, as they sometimes forget to swallow, and instead stash the food in their cheeks.

✳ TIP
For a finger food feast, offer cooked broccoli florets or sticks of cooked carrot.

pumpkin and rosemary breadsticks

Homemade breadsticks are ideal for a teething baby. Freeze them, thawing a few at a time – they take about 30 minutes to defrost at room temperature.

MAKES 60

4 tablespoons pumpkin seeds

4 tablespoons olive oil

750 g (1½ lb) strong white bread flour, plus extra for dusting

7 g (¼ oz) sachet easy-blend dried yeast

2 tender stems of fresh rosemary, leaves very finely chopped

about 500 ml (17 fl oz) lukewarm water

✶ TIP
Delicious served with Mixed Vegetable Dip (see page 60).

FOR OLDER BABIES AND TODDLERS
Serve the breadsticks with dips that are suitable for the age of your child, so he becomes accustomed to a range of different tastes.

1 Dry-fry the pumpkin seeds in a small heavy-based frying pan over a medium heat for about 1 minute, until lightly toasted. Grind the toasted seeds with 2 tablespoons of the oil to a smooth paste in a clean spice or coffee grinder or with a pestle and mortar.

2 Sift the flour into a bowl, add the pumpkin seed paste, yeast and rosemary, then mix in enough water to form a soft, but not sticky dough. Knead vigorously on a well-floured surface, then cut the dough into 60 pieces. Roll each piece into a 20 cm- (8 inch-) long rope.

3 Lay the dough sticks on 2 large, oiled baking trays, spacing them slightly apart. Brush lightly with the remaining olive oil and cover loosely with clingfilm. Leave in a warm place for about 20 minutes, or until well risen. Remove the clingfilm.

4 Bake the breadsticks in a preheated oven at 220°C (425°F), Gas Mark 7 for 8–10 minutes, transposing the trays after 5 minutes to ensure even cooking. Transfer the breadsticks to wire racks to cool.

5 Put a few breadsticks in an airtight container and use within 24 hours. Pack the rest into freezer bags or one large plastic container, seal and freeze for up to six weeks. Take out a few at a time as required.

cheese straws

These popular snacks are healthier than biscuits or crisps, especially if served with raw vegetables.

MAKES 50

125 g (4 oz) plain white flour, plus extra for dusting

50 g (2 oz) unsalted butter, diced

75 g (3 oz) mild Cheddar cheese, grated

1 egg yolk

1 egg, beaten

* TIP
You can use half white and half wholemeal flour if you wish.

FOR OLDER BABIES AND TODDLERS
Sprinkle the cheese straws with sesame seeds before you bake them.

Try cutting into interesting shapes, letters or simple animals with biscuit cutters.

1 Put the flour into a bowl, add the butter and rub in with your fingertips or an electric mixer until it resembles fine breadcrumbs. Stir in the cheese. Mix the egg yolk with 1 tablespoon of the beaten egg, stir into the flour and bring together to form a smooth, soft dough.

2 Knead lightly on a floured surface, then roll out to about 3 mm (⅛ inch) thick. Cut into 1 x 5 cm (½ x 2 inch) strips. Brush with the remaining beaten egg, separate the straws and place on a baking sheet, spaced slightly apart.

3 Bake in a preheated oven at 200°C (400°F), Gas Mark 6 for 8–10 minutes, until golden. Leave to cool on the baking sheets.

4 Store in a plastic box and use within two days or freeze for up to six weeks.

tiddler's tortilla

This simple tortilla can easily be adapted to include a little diced red pepper, sweetcorn, diced courgette and a few sliced mushrooms.

2–3 SERVINGS

2 teaspoons vegetable oil

125 g (4 oz) cooked potato, diced

2 tablespoons frozen mixed vegetables, large pieces chopped

½ spring onion, finely chopped

2 eggs

2 tablespoons grated Cheddar cheese

✳ TIP
Don't be tempted to add salt and pepper to foods for children under one. Add flavour with a little finely chopped onion, a few herbs or a little garlic instead.

FOR OLDER BABIES AND TODDLERS
Older children may prefer their omelette with baked beans or ketchup, but either make your own (see page 96) or choose brands free from salt and sugar.

1 Heat the oil in a 15 cm (6 inch) nonstick frying pan. Add the potato and frozen vegetables and fry over a gentle heat for 5 minutes, until the potatoes are browned and the frozen vegetables are hot. Add the chopped onion and cook for 1 more minute.

2 Beat the eggs with the cheese. Pour the egg mixture into the pan and cook until the underside is golden. Place the pan under a preheated grill, making sure the pan handle is away from the heat, and cook until the top of the omelette is golden and the eggs are thoroughly cooked.

3 Loosen the edge of the omelette, slide it on to a chopping board and cut into pieces. Spoon-feed your baby or serve as finger food.

mini apple custard pots

Naturally sweetened with a little poached fruit, these small baked custards are made with basic ingredients from the larder, refrigerator and fruit bowl.

2 SERVINGS

1 dessert apple, peeled, cored and chopped

1 tablespoon water

pinch of ground cinnamon

butter, for greasing

1 egg

150 ml (¼ pint) full-fat milk

1 Put the apple into a small saucepan with the water and cinnamon. Cover and cook gently for 5 minutes, until the apple is soft.

2 Butter 2 ramekins or other small ovenproof dishes and divide the poached apple between them.

3 Lightly beat the egg in a bowl. Heat the milk in a saucepan until just below boiling point, then gradually beat it into the egg. Strain the custard over the poached apple in the ramekins.

4 Stand the ramekins in a small roasting tin. Add boiling water to the tin to come halfway up the sides of the dishes. Bake in a preheated oven at 180°C (350°F), Gas Mark 4, for 20–25 minutes until the custard is set and feels quite firm to the touch. If it is at all wobbly, return to the oven for a further 5 minutes.

5 Allow to cool before serving. Use the second portion within 24 hours.

✳ TIP
The custards are not suitable for freezing.

FOR OLDER BABIES AND TODDLERS
Mix in other fruits that you are introducing to your child, such as apricots or blueberries.

prune and banana sundae

If you have a small, hand-held electric baby blender, you can whizz up this delicious, naturally sweet dessert in seconds.

1 SERVING

3 ready-to-eat pitted prunes, about 25 g (1 oz)

1 tablespoon fresh orange juice

½ small banana, sliced

2 tablespoons natural bio yogurt

1 Blend the prunes and orange juice together until finely chopped.

2 Add the banana and yogurt and blend briefly, then spoon into a small bowl and serve. Give your baby a spoon, too, so that he can practise feeding himself.

✳ TIP
This is such a quick and simple pudding to make that you can easily prepare a single portion as you need it.

FOR OLDER BABIES AND TODDLERS
Don't blend the prunes too finely – leave slightly chunky so your child needs to chew them.

toddlers

Once the foundations for a healthy diet are laid, your toddler should be enjoying a wide range of foods with a variety of textures and tastes. The following recipes will continue to broaden your child's diet and give them lots of energy.

adapting recipes for babies

Some of the recipes in the following section include a tip box 'Okay for under-ones?' which gives advice on whether the recipe is suitable for a younger child. It also gives suggestions on changing the texture of the meal to suit different stages of development, together with alternative ingredients where applicable.

recipe contents

finger fruits with yogurt

Dipping fruit into creamy yogurt has great appeal for young children. Ring the changes with fresh strawberries, raspberries or pineapple.

4–6 SERVINGS

1–2 apples or pears

1 orange

1 mango

½ small pineapple (optional)

1–2 bananas

475 ml (16 fl oz) natural bio yogurt

a little muscovado sugar, to taste (optional)

1 Quarter and core the apples or pears, peel if preferred and cut into long slices. Peel the orange and divide into segments. Peel the mango and cut the flesh away from the stone, then slice. Peel the pineapple and slice into rings or sticks, cutting out the central core. Peel and halve the bananas.

2 Arrange the 'finger fruits' on individual plates with a small bowl of yogurt. Serve the muscovado sugar separately.

OKAY FOR UNDER-ONES?
6–12 months Use unsweetened yogurt and omit the muscovado sugar. Blend or mash the fruit with yogurt until your baby is able to chew, then cut it into small pieces or sticks that they can hold.

* TIP
Give under-twos whole-fat yogurt; 2–5-year-olds can have either whole- or half-fat yogurt.

baby bear's big breakfast

A bowl of comforting, warm porridge makes a sustaining breakfast which can be enhanced with fresh, cooked or dried fruit, or a little honey or jam.

4–6 SERVINGS

125 g (4 oz) quick-cook porridge oats

1.2 litres (2 pints) full-fat milk or water

to serve

4 ripe bananas, thinly sliced, or 75 g (3 oz) sultanas or chopped dried dates, or 250 g (8 oz) stewed apricots

a little honey or apricot or cherry jam (optional)

1 Put the porridge oats and milk or water into a large saucepan and bring to the boil. Simmer, stirring occasionally, for about 5 minutes, until thickened.

2 Divide the porridge between serving bowls. Add fruit, as well as honey or jam if you wish.

OKAY FOR UNDER-ONES?
6–12 months Make the porridge with whole milk. Don't give honey. Mash the bananas well, or purée sultanas, dates or apricots. When your baby can cope with lumps, cut the fruit into small pieces or sticks. Clean your baby's teeth and gums afterwards.

✳ TIP
Porridge made with milk rather than water is creamier and sweeter, although some children prefer milk-free porridge.

pocket omelette

Stuff a pitta bread with a folded-over vegetable omelette and you have the perfect fortifying breakfast.

4–6 SERVINGS

1 tablespoon vegetable oil

2 carrots, grated, or 4 tomatoes, chopped, or 125 g (4 oz) cabbage, spinach or pak choi, chopped

6 eggs

4 pitta breads

black pepper

1 Heat the oil in a large frying pan, add the carrots, tomatoes, cabbage or other greens, and cook for 2–3 minutes until they start to soften.

2 Meanwhile, break the eggs into a bowl, add a little pepper, and beat with a fork until smooth and frothy.

3 Pour the egg mixture over the vegetables in the pan, and quickly mix together using a wooden spoon. Cook, without stirring, until the top is set. Lift the edges of the omelette to allow the uncooked egg to run underneath and cook. Pop under the grill to lightly brown the top.

4 Warm the pitta breads briefly in the toaster or microwave, or under the grill; do not overheat or they will become brittle. Open each along one long side.

5 Cut the omelette into wedges, roll each one loosely, then place in an opened pitta pocket. Serve hot or warm, with homemade tomato ketchup if you like.

OKAY FOR UNDER-ONES?
6–9 months Blend the food with a little milk or water. Or, when your baby can chew, cut into small pieces and add a little milk or water to soften the bread. Some babies like to hold a piece of pitta bread.

9–12 months Cut the pitta bread up small, or give your baby a piece to hold.

✳ TIP
Mini pitta breads are available and are useful for those with smaller appetites; alternatively, an ordinary pitta can be halved.

drop scones

These delicious little flat scones are quick and easy to cook and unbelievably moreish, especially with a topping to tantalize the tastebuds.

4–6 SERVINGS

250 g (8 oz) plain flour

1 teaspoon bicarbonate of soda

2 teaspoons cream of tartar

1 tablespoon caster sugar

2 eggs

1 teaspoon vegetable oil

300 ml (½ pint) full-fat milk

unsalted butter, for frying

75 g (3 oz) blueberries

2 tablespoons water

75 g (3 oz) Greek yogurt

OKAY FOR UNDER-ONES?
Omit the bicarbonate of soda; this will slightly alter the texture.

6–9 months Either blend a scone and its topping with a little milk or water or, once your baby can chew, cut up the scone and topping and soften with a little milk or water.

9–12 months Cut up the scone and topping, or let your baby hold a piece of it.

1 Put the flour, bicarbonate of soda, cream of tartar and sugar in a bowl and make a well in the centre. Add the eggs, oil and half of the milk to the well, and gradually incorporate the flour with a whisk. Add the remaining milk and whisk well to make a smooth batter.

2 For the topping, put the blueberries and water in a small pan and cook gently for 2–3 minutes to soften slightly.

3 Melt a small knob of butter in a large non-stick frying pan. Cook the scones in batches. Drop large spoonfuls of batter into the pan from the tip of a spoon to form rounds, spacing well apart. Cook for 2–3 minutes until bubbles appear on the surface and burst, then turn them over and cook for a further 1–2 minutes until golden brown underneath. Put the scones on a clean tea towel and fold it over to keep them warm, while cooking the rest.

4 Serve the scones warm, either plain or topped with a spoonful of the blueberry compote and a dollop of yogurt.

✳ TIP
Use buttermilk rather than ordinary milk, reducing the cream of tartar to 1 teaspoon.

curly coconut pasta

This combination of chicken, broccoli and pasta is popular with children of all ages, partly because the coconut lends a touch of sweetness.

4–6 SERVINGS

250–375 g (8–12 oz) pasta spirals

500 g (1 lb) broccoli florets

1 tablespoon vegetable oil

1 shallot or small onion, chopped

1 garlic clove, chopped

small pinch of chilli powder (optional)

250 g (8 oz) cooked skinless, boneless chicken, cut into bite-sized pieces

4 tablespoons crème fraîche

½–1 teaspoon Dijon mustard (optional)

50 g (2 oz) creamed coconut, grated

black pepper

1 Cook the pasta in a large saucepan of boiling water for about 10 minutes until al dente – tender but firm to the bite. At the same time, cook the broccoli in a steamer until just tender.

2 Meanwhile, heat the oil in a large frying pan, add the onion and fry for about 5 minutes until lightly browned. Add the garlic and chilli powder, if using, and fry for a further minute. Add the chicken, crème fraîche, mustard, if using, coconut and pepper. Heat through, stirring.

3 Drain the pasta spirals and stir into the sauce. Finally, stir in the cooked broccoli florets, taking care not to break them up too much.

OKAY FOR UNDER-ONES?
6–12 months Omit the chilli and mustard. In a blender, process the pasta with a little sauce. Once your baby can cope with lumps, cut the pasta up small.

✳ TIP
If you're not cooking for under-ones, and your family likes spicy flavours, use ½ teaspoon of chilli powder and 2 teaspoons of mustard.

chicken casserole

A chicken casserole can be assembled quickly, popped into the oven, then forgotten while you do something else. It is easily adapted for babies.

4–6 SERVINGS

4 chicken quarters or breasts

2 tablespoons plain flour

2 tablespoons vegetable oil

2 leeks, trimmed and chopped

2 carrots, sliced

1–2 garlic cloves, crushed

3–4 turnips, cut into 2.5 cm (1 inch) chunks

2 tablespoons small red lentils

2 teaspoons chopped fresh mixed herbs such as parsley, oregano and thyme

1 litre (1¾ pints) homemade chicken stock (see page 126) or water

black pepper

75 ml (3 fl oz) single cream or crème fraîche (optional)

OKAY FOR UNDER-ONES?
6–12 months Remove any bones. If not using homemade stock, use salt-free stock. Blend the vegetables and chicken.

1 Toss the chicken pieces in the flour to coat evenly, shaking off the excess.

2 Heat the oil in a heavy-based casserole, add the leeks and carrots, and cook gently for 7–8 minutes, stirring occasionally, until softened. Remove with a slotted spoon and set aside.

3 Add the chicken pieces and garlic to the casserole and cook for 8–10 minutes, turning the chicken occasionally to brown on all sides.

4 Add the turnips, lentils, herbs and pepper, then return the sautéed vegetables to the casserole. Pour in the chicken stock or water and bring to the boil.

5 Cover the casserole and cook in a preheated oven at 180°C (350°F), Gas Mark 4 for 1¼ hours. Remove from the oven and stir in the cream or crème fraîche, if using.

6 Serve accompanied by boiled rice (preferably brown), or steamed or baked sweet potatoes, and peas.

✳ TIP
This dish freezes well, so you could make double and freeze half for another occasion.

chicken risi bisi

Add chicken to the classic rice and peas and you have a flavourful risotto. Carrots, broccoli, peas, broad beans and sweetcorn also work well.

4 SERVINGS

25 g (1 oz) unsalted butter

1 tablespoon vegetable oil

2 large skinless, boneless chicken breasts, cut into chunks

1 onion, chopped

1 garlic clove, crushed

400 g (13 oz) arborio or other risotto rice (preferably brown)

1.2 litres (2 pints) homemade vegetable stock or chicken stock (see page 126)

150 g (5 oz) mangetout, cut diagonally into 2.5 cm (1 inch) lengths

50 g (2 oz) Parmesan or Cheddar cheese, grated (optional)

1 Melt the butter with the oil in a large, heavy-based saucepan. Add the chicken and fry gently for about 5 minutes until cooked through. Remove with a slotted spoon.

2 Add the onion and garlic to the pan and fry gently for 2 minutes. Stir in the rice and cook for 1 minute.

3 Add a ladleful of stock and cook, stirring, until absorbed. Add about two thirds of the remaining stock and cook gently, stirring frequently. Once the stock is almost absorbed and the rice is nearly tender, return the chicken to the pan with the mangetout and remaining stock.

4 Cook for a further 5 minutes or until the rice is tender, adding a little more stock if the mixture becomes dry. Stir in the cheese, if using, to serve.

OKAY FOR UNDER-ONES?
6–12 months Blend the food for younger babies who can't cope with lumps; by about 10 months most babies can chew chicken if it's cut up very small.

✳ TIP
A 'classic' risotto is made by adding the stock to the pan a little at a time, stirring continuously, and adding more stock once it has been absorbed. This risotto is simpler and the results are equally good.

vegetable and chicken stir-fry

Stir-frying makes vegetables taste more attractive – even to the most reluctant child – because it brings out their natural sweetness.

4–6 SERVINGS

175 g (6 oz) baby carrots, scraped

175 g (6 oz) baby corn, halved lengthways

3 tablespoons vegetable oil

500 g (1 lb) skinless, boneless chicken breast, cut into thin strips across the grain

1 red pepper, cored, deseeded and thinly sliced lengthways

1 garlic clove, crushed

175 g (6 oz) small mangetout

✳ TIP
For over-ones, try adding up to 4 tablespoons of yellow bean sauce and 1 tablespoon of sherry vinegar before returning the chicken.

OKAY FOR UNDER-ONES?
6–12 months Blend or mince the stir-fry until your baby is able to chew small pieces of chicken, baby corn and mangetout – probably around 10 months, then cut the food up small.

1 Blanch the carrots in boiling water for 2 minutes. Lift out with a slotted spoon, immediately refresh under cold running water, then drain. Repeat with the baby corn.

2 Heat 2 tablespoons of the oil in a wok or large, deep frying pan over a moderate heat. Add the chicken strips, increase the heat to high and stir-fry for 3–4 minutes or until lightly coloured on all sides. Remove the chicken with a slotted spoon and set aside.

3 Heat the remaining oil in the wok on a moderate heat. Add the red pepper and garlic and stir-fry for 2–3 minutes until softened, but not coloured.

4 Add the vegetables, increase the heat to high and stir-fry for 3–4 minutes, until lightly browned. Add the chicken and its juices and toss over the heat for 1 minute. Serve with rice.

chicken and vegetable pies

There's something about wrapping food in pastry that makes it more appealing, and children of all ages will love these tasty filo pies.

MAKES 10

50 g (2 oz) unsalted butter

2 large skinless, boneless chicken breasts, cut into small cubes

1 large leek, trimmed and chopped

150 g (5 oz) carrots, thinly sliced

2 teaspoons plain flour

200 ml (7 fl oz) homemade chicken stock (see page 126)

100 g (3½ oz) French beans, sliced

4 tablespoons double cream

175 g (6 oz) ready-made filo pastry

OKAY FOR UNDER-ONES?
6–12 months Blend the food for younger babies who can't yet cope with lumps. By about 10 months most babies will manage to chew diced chicken, so you can cut the pies into small pieces.

1 Melt 25 g (1 oz) of the butter in a large frying pan. Fry the chicken for 3 minutes until lightly browned. Add the leek and carrots and fry for 2 minutes until softened. Stir in the flour.

2 Stir in the stock, then add the French beans. Bring to the boil, stirring. Cover and cook for 5 minutes. Stir in the cream and leave to cool.

3 Melt the remaining butter. Cut the pastry into thirty 13 cm (5 inch) squares. Lightly brush one square with butter, cover with another square and brush with butter. Add a third square and brush the edges with butter. Place a heaped dessertspoon of filling in the centre. Bring up the corners of the pastry over the filling and pinch the edges together to form an envelope. Repeat with the remaining filling and pastry to make 10 pies.

4 Place the pies on a lightly greased baking sheet and brush with the remaining butter. Bake in a preheated oven at 200°C (400°F), Gas Mark 6 for 15–20 minutes, or until golden brown. Serve with creamy mashed potato and carrots.

✳ TIP
If you have any leftover pies, they are handy for a packed lunch or to take on a picnic the next day.

toad 'n' roots in the hole

Tasty roasted root vegetables are incorporated into this delicious variation of traditional toad-in-the-hole.

4–6 SERVINGS

375 g (12 oz) raw beetroot

2 carrots

2 onions, quartered

3 tablespoons vegetable oil

8 sausages

8 rashers of streaky bacon

125 g (4 oz) plain flour

1 egg

300 ml (½ pint) full-fat milk

✳ TIPS

Use quality butcher's-style sausages and experiment with different flavours.

For a vegetarian option, omit the sausages and add to the vegetables, using parsnips and leeks, for example.

OKAY FOR UNDER-ONES?
6–12 months Omit the bacon and sausages. Blend the cooked vegetables and batter with a little milk or water. Or, cut up small and moisten, if necessary, with milk or water.

1 Scrub the beetroot and cut the beetroot and carrots into 4 cm (1½ inch) chunks. Put in a roasting tin with the onions, drizzle with the oil and toss to coat. Roast in a preheated oven at 190°C (375°F), Gas Mark 5 for 25 minutes.

2 Meanwhile, prick the sausages with a fork and wrap a bacon rasher around each one.

3 Remove the roasting tin from the oven, turn the vegetables, add the bacon-wrapped sausages and turn them to coat with oil. Roast for a further 10 minutes.

4 Meanwhile, make the batter. Put the flour into a bowl and stir in the egg and half the milk. Whisk in the remaining milk until smooth.

5 Turn the sausages and spread them and the vegetables evenly in the roasting tin. Pour in the batter, return to the oven and bake for a further 40 minutes until the batter is well risen and crisp. Serve with peas or cabbage and baked beans if you like.

silly sausages

Serve sausages in an original way to give them a little more child-appeal. Look for good-quality sausages that have a high percentage of lean meat.

4 SERVINGS

750 g (1½ lb) potatoes, peeled and chopped

a little full-fat milk

8 good-quality sausages

1–2 tablespoons vegetable oil

✳ TIP
Sausages are typically high in fat, so choose low-fat sausages and cut down the fat content of the rest of the meal. They are also high in salt, so don't feed them to your toddler too often.

OKAY FOR UNDER-ONES?
6–12 months Only sausages without added salt are suitable. If available, either blend cooked sausages and potato with some milk or water or, once your baby can chew, cut up small. Don't give canned baked beans or ready-made tomato ketchup.

1 Cook the potatoes in a saucepan of boiling water until tender. Drain and mash thoroughly with a little milk.

2 Meanwhile, prick each sausage with a fork in 3 places. Heat the oil in a non-stick frying pan, add the sausages and fry, turning occasionally, for 10–20 minutes, depending on thickness, until cooked through.

3 Cut each sausage in half widthways. Make a mound of mashed potato on each plate, then stick 4 sausage halves into each mound, cut end downwards. Serve with green beans, broccoli, peas or baked beans.

popeye's pork

Although spinach contains iron, it is not the best source. A higher level was mistakenly assigned to spinach in a nutrient table some time ago.

4–6 SERVINGS

500 g (1 lb) small red 'salad' potatoes, scrubbed

500 g (1 lb) pork escalopes

2 tablespoons vegetable oil

1 red onion, chopped

1 garlic clove, crushed

150 ml (¼ pint) homemade vegetable stock or chicken stock (see page 126)

175 g (6 oz) fromage frais

200 g (7 oz) baby spinach, trimmed and washed

1 Halve any large potatoes to give even-sized chunks. Steam over boiling water for 15 minutes until just tender. Meanwhile, press the pork between pieces of kitchen paper to remove excess moisture, then cut into thin strips.

2 Heat the oil in a large frying pan or wok. Add the pork and fry quickly for about 3 minutes, until cooked through. Add the onion and garlic and fry, stirring, for a further 3–4 minutes until softened.

3 Add the stock and fromage frais. Cover and simmer gently for 5 minutes. Add the potatoes and spinach and cook gently, stirring the spinach into the cooking juices until wilted. Serve immediately.

OKAY FOR UNDER-ONES?
6–12 months Cut the cooked pork up small, then blend all the food together. Alternatively, for babies who can cope with lumps, mince the pork and mash the rest. Your baby will probably be around 10 months before he or she can chew little pieces of pork, however small you cut them.

✳ TIPS
Yellow-skinned potatoes are a good alternative to red ones. The skins of both red and yellow-skinned potatoes contain more plant pigments than do those of ordinary 'white' potatoes.

Beetroot is a good accompaniment to this dish: simply boil raw beetroot until soft, rub off their skins, then grate to serve.

hot cats

Fast foods, such as burgers and hot dogs, are perennial favourites. Create your own fun versions for everyone to eat with their fingers.

4 SERVINGS

4 pieces of fresh skinless cod, each 75 g (3 oz), or frozen fish steaks, thawed

4 long, soft rolls or 4 baps

2 tablespoons mayonnaise

2 tablespoons Greek yogurt

handful of Romaine or Cos lettuce leaves

1 large or 2 small gherkins, sliced (optional)

1 Steam the fish in a steamer or poach in a shallow pan containing a 1 cm (½ inch) depth of simmering water for 8–10 minutes until just tender.

2 Split open the rolls or baps, but do not cut right through. Mix the mayonnaise and yogurt together in a small bowl, then spread on the cut surfaces of each roll or bap.

3 Lay 1 or 2 lettuce leaves on the bottom half of each roll, add a few gherkin slices, if using, then insert the fish fillets, cutting to fit as necessary.

4 Serve with green beans or peas, oven-baked chips and homemade tomato ketchup.

OKAY FOR UNDER-ONES?
6–12 months Check fish carefully for bones, even though it is sold as filleted. Blend with a little milk or water or, once your baby can chew, cut up small and moisten if necessary with a little milk or water.

✴ TIPS
You can grill or bake the fish if preferred, but steaming or poaching keeps it moist.

For a more piquant flavour, you can replace 1 tablespoon of the mayonnaise with 1 tablespoon of tartare sauce (not for under-ones).

fish pie

In this tasty pie the light texture of the fish and smooth root mash contrast well with the crisp breadcrumb topping. Great with peas or spring greens.

6–8 SERVINGS

500 g (1 lb) potatoes, cubed

500 g (1 lb) swede, cubed

625 g (1¼ lb) fresh cod, haddock, ling or salmon fillets

450 ml (¾ pint) full-fat milk

25 g (1 oz) unsalted butter

1 leek, rinsed, trimmed and finely sliced

25 g (1 oz) plain flour

75 g (3 oz) bread, crusts removed

2 teaspoons chopped fresh parsley or chervil

black pepper

> **✳ TIP**
> If fresh fish isn't available, use frozen fish fillets or canned salmon.

OKAY FOR UNDER-ONES?
6–12 months Check the fish carefully for bones. Blend the fish and vegetable mash with a little milk or water, or cut up small and mash with the topping.

1 Cook the potatoes and swede in boiling water for 15–20 minutes, or until soft. Steam the fish fillets, or poach in water to cover for 12 minutes. Drain potatoes and swede thoroughly. Mash with a third of the milk, and pepper to taste.

2 Melt the butter in a saucepan, cook the leek for 5–6 minutes, until softened. Stir in the flour and cook for 1 minute, then stir in the milk, to make a smooth sauce. Take off the heat.

3 Flake the fish, making sure all bones are removed, then add to the sauce. Spread in the base of a greased, shallow ovenproof dish.

4 Put the bread and herbs in a blender or food processor and process briefly to make herby breadcrumbs. Spoon the mash over the fish, then scatter the herby breadcrumbs on top. Bake in a preheated oven at 190°C (375°F), Gas Mark 5 for 25–30 minutes, until golden brown.

fish stir-fry

White fish is excellent for babies and toddlers. The subtle flavours from the mild chilli sauce, orange juice and vegetables make this a delicious stir-fry.

4–6 SERVINGS

375 g (12 oz) fresh cod or haddock fillets, skinned

2 teaspoons cornflour

75 ml (3 fl oz) freshly squeezed orange juice

1 tablespoon mild sweet chilli sauce

3 medium carrots

3–4 spring onions

4 Chinese leaves or spring greens

1 red pepper, halved, cored and deseeded

200 g (7 oz) medium egg noodles

3 tablespoons vegetable oil

75 g (3 oz) frozen peas

OKAY FOR UNDER-ONES?
6–12 months Blend for younger babies who can't cope with lumps; cut up the noodles and mash the fish for older babies.

1 Cut the fish into small chunks and toss in the cornflour to coat. Mix any remaining cornflour with the orange juice and chilli sauce.

2 Shred the carrots, spring onions, Chinese leaves or greens and red pepper, using the shredder attachment of a food processor. Alternatively slice the vegetables very thinly.

3 Cook the egg noodles in a saucepan of boiling water according to the packet instructions.

4 Heat the oil in a large frying pan or wok. Add the shredded vegetables and stir-fry for about 3 minutes, until softened but still retaining their texture. Remove with a slotted spoon and set aside. Add the fish to the saucepan and stir-fry for 3 minutes until cooked through. Return the vegetables to the saucepan. Add the peas and chilli sauce mixture, and heat through for 1 minute, stirring gently.

5 Drain the noodles and transfer to serving bowls. Spoon the stir-fry on top and serve.

✷ TIP
If you're short of time, use a bag of ready prepared stir-fry vegetables.

salmon and pasta salad

Salmon is a three-way winner. First, its colour will boost a child's appetite. Second, it's easy to eat. And third, it's a good source of omega-3 fats.

4–6 SERVINGS

250 g (8 oz) fresh salmon fillet

15 g (½ oz) unsalted butter

200 g (7 oz) tricolour fusilli, or other pasta shapes

150 g (5 oz) mangetout, thinly sliced

1 ripe avocado

2 tomatoes, peeled, deseeded and finely chopped

4 tablespoons natural bio yogurt

2–3 teaspoons chopped fresh chives or mint

> **✳ TIP**
> The salmon can be gently poached or cooked in the microwave if preferred.

> **OKAY FOR UNDER-ONES?**
> **6–12 months** Check very carefully for fish bones. Blend for younger babies who can't chew. Cut up the pasta, salmon and mangetout for older children.

1 Put the salmon on a foil-lined grill rack and dot with the butter. Cook under a preheated moderate grill for about 8 minutes until cooked through. Leave to cool.

2 Meanwhile, cook the pasta in a saucepan of boiling water until almost *al dente* – tender but firm to the bite. Add the mangetout and cook for a further 1 minute. Drain the pasta and mangetout and refresh under cold water.

3 Flake the fish, discarding the skin and making sure any bones are removed. Halve, stone and peel the avocado, then cut into small dice. Toss the pasta, mangetout, flaked salmon, avocado and tomatoes together in a bowl.

4 Mix the yogurt with the herbs. Drizzle over the pasta salad to serve.

cowboy beans

This version of the ever-popular baked beans has the advantage that you know exactly what is in it – standard baked beans are high in sugar and salt.

4 SERVINGS

175 g (6 oz) dried pinto, borlotti or cannellini beans, soaked in cold water overnight

1 bay leaf

1 tablespoon vegetable oil

1 onion, finely chopped

1 garlic clove, crushed

1 tablespoon plain flour

1 teaspoon paprika

300 ml (½ pint) homemade vegetable stock (see page 126)

1 tablespoon tomato purée

1 tablespoon brown sugar

black pepper (optional)

slaw

1 small banana, sliced

1 small orange, peeled and segmented

1 small dessert apple, cored and diced

75 g (3 oz) red cabbage, cored and finely shredded

3 tablespoons sprouted alfalfa seeds, rinsed

1 Drain the beans, rinse with cold water, then put into a saucepan with the bay leaf. Cover with plenty of fresh cold water. Bring to the boil and boil rapidly for 10 minutes. Skim off any scum from the surface and simmer for 1 hour or until tender.

2 Heat the oil in a frying pan, add the onion and garlic and fry for 5 minutes, stirring until golden. Stir in the flour and paprika and cook for 1 minute, then stir in the stock, tomato purée and sugar. Season lightly if required.

3 Drain the cooked beans, return to the saucepan and stir in the sauce. Bring to the boil, cover and simmer for 15 minutes.

4 Meanwhile, toss all the slaw ingredients together in a bowl. Spoon the beans into serving bowls and top with the slaw.

OKAY FOR UNDER-ONES?
6–9 months Not suitable.

9–12 months Mash plain boiled beans with boiled potato and carrot and flavour with a little tomato purée, fresh, skinned, deseeded tomatoes or a little crushed garlic.

✳ TIP
You can freeze the beans in portions, without the slaw topping, for up to six weeks

bean and feta falafel

These little spicy patties are popular with young and old alike. Here they are made with frozen broad beans for speed, and mixed with a little feta.

2–3 SERVINGS

150 g (5 oz) frozen baby broad beans

½ small onion, roughly chopped

½ teaspoon ground cumin

1 teaspoon ground coriander

50 g (2 oz) feta cheese, chopped

a little plain flour

2 tablespoons vegetable oil

6 mini pitta breads

1 Little Gem lettuce, roughly torn

3 tablespoons natural bio yogurt

little finely chopped fresh mint (optional)

¼ cucumber, sliced

1 dessert apple, cored and sliced

OKAY FOR UNDER-ONES?
6–9 months Purée small amounts of broad beans with other vegetables. Reduce the spices and blend in grated cheese.

9–12 months Finely chop or process the broad beans Serve with strips of pitta.

1 Put the broad beans into a saucepan of boiling water and simmer for 4 minutes then drain.

2 Put the beans into a food processor with the onion, spices and feta, and process until finely chopped. Or finely chop all the ingredients by hand and mix in a bowl.

3 Divide the mixture into 6 portions, then press into small oval patties between well-floured hands. Heat the oil in a frying pan and fry for 5 minutes, turning several times until golden.

4 Meanwhile, warm the pitta breads in the oven or under the grill.

5 Split the pitta breads open, pop a little lettuce and a falafel into each one, then spoon in a little plain yogurt, or yogurt flavoured with chopped mint. Serve with cucumber and apple slices.

big bean burgers

These tasty vegetarian burgers look just like standard burgers. Serve with a few oven chips and homemade tomato ketchup.

2 SERVINGS

2 teaspoons vegetable oil

1 small onion

1 small garlic clove, crushed

1 teaspoon ground cumin

1 teaspoon ground coriander

½ teaspoon paprika

300 g (10 oz) can black eye beans, drained and rinsed

a little flour

to serve

2 small soft rolls

few cucumber slices

1 tomato, sliced

a little tomato ketchup

1 Heat half of the oil in a frying pan. Add the onion and garlic and fry, stirring occasionally, for 4–5 minutes until lightly browned. Stir in the spices and cook for 1 minute.

2 Drain the beans, then add to the onion mixture. Mash or briefly process in a blender. Divide the mixture in half and shape each portion into a burger, using well-floured hands.

3 Heat the remaining oil in the clean frying pan and fry the burgers for 3–4 minutes on each side until browned.

4 Split the rolls and arrange the cucumber and tomato slices on the bases. Add the burgers and a little ketchup. Sandwich together with the top halves of the rolls and serve.

OKAY FOR UNDER-ONES?
6–9 months Not suitable.

9–12 months Give tiny pieces of burger and strips of bread roll as finger food, along with a little peeled cucumber and pieces of deseeded tomato. Do not serve with ketchup.

✳ TIPS
Cook your own beans and freeze. For this recipe you need 200 g (7 oz) cooked weight.

Chickpeas or a mixture of red and white kidney beans work well.

stripy macaroni cheese

Make this quick and easy pasta dish in heatproof glass dishes so that your children can see and count the different layers.

2 SERVINGS

125 g (4 oz) macaroni

100 g (3½ oz) broccoli, cut into tiny florets, stems sliced

1 carrot, about 125 g (4 oz), peeled and sliced

50 g (2 oz) frozen sweetcorn

15 g (½ oz) unsalted butter

15 g (½ oz) plain flour

200 ml (7 fl oz) full-fat milk

100 g (3½ oz) medium Cheddar cheese, grated

1 tablespoon fresh breadcrumbs

to serve

quartered cherry tomatoes

OKAY FOR UNDER-ONES?
6–9 months Omit the sweetcorn as it is difficult for a young baby to digest. Purée the mixture with extra milk to the desired texture.

9–12 months Finely chop or mash the food to the required texture.

1 Cook the macaroni in a saucepan of boiling water until *al dente* – tender but firm to the bite. Meanwhile, cook the broccoli, carrot and sweetcorn in a steamer for 6–7 minutes.

2 Meanwhile, melt the butter in a saucepan. Stir in the flour and cook for 1 minute, then gradually mix in the milk and bring to the boil, stirring until thick and smooth. Stir in three-quarters of the cheese.

3 Drain the pasta and stir into the sauce. Spoon two-thirds of the macaroni cheese into two 200 ml (7 fl oz) individual ovenproof dishes. Arrange the vegetables in layers on top, then cover with the rest of the macaroni cheese.

4 Sprinkle with the remaining cheese and breadcrumbs and brown under a preheated hot grill for 5 minutes. Leave to cool slightly before serving with cherry tomatoes.

easy peasy lasagne

Green peas contrast well with golden sweetcorn to create a colourful dish that is popular with young children.

4–6 SERVINGS

50 g (2 oz) unsalted butter

2 onions, chopped

2 garlic cloves, crushed

50 g (2 oz) plain flour

600 ml (1 pint) vegetable stock

300 ml (½ pint) full-fat milk

black pepper

375 g (12 oz) fresh green peas

250 g (8 oz) can sweetcorn (preferably without salt or sugar), drained

1 tablespoon chopped fresh parsley or mint

150 g (5 oz) ready-to-cook lasagne verdi sheets

OKAY FOR UNDER-ONES?

6–12 months If not using homemade stock, make sure it is salt-free. Once your baby can chew, cut the food up small. If beans and onions make your baby windy, serve for lunch rather than supper.

1 Melt the butter in a saucepan, add the onions and cook gently until soft. Add the garlic and fry for a few minutes. Stir in the flour and cook for about 1 minute. Slowly pour in the stock and milk, stirring all the time. Bring the sauce slowly to the boil, stirring constantly until thickened and smooth. Season with pepper.

2 Shell the peas if necessary, then par-cook them in boiling water for 4–5 minutes and drain. Combine with the sweetcorn in a bowl and stir in the parsley or mint.

3 Pour a third of the sauce into a shallow ovenproof dish, then cover with a layer of lasagne sheets. Spoon the pea and sweetcorn mixture over the lasagne, then cover with half of the remaining sauce. Lay the remaining lasagne sheets on top and pour on the remaining sauce.

4 Bake in a preheated oven at 190°C (375°F), Gas Mark 5 for about 25 minutes until the top is golden brown and bubbling. Serve with spinach, peas or green beans.

* TIP
Make the sauce with vegetable rather than chicken stock and you have a meal suitable for vegetarians.

autumn pasta

Butternut squash gives this recipe its harvest-gold colour and, as the name suggests, it tastes both buttery and nutty.

4–6 SERVINGS

375–425 g (12–14 oz) pasta shapes

25 g (1 oz) unsalted butter

2 tablespoons vegetable oil

500 g (1 lb) butternut squash, peeled, deseeded and cut into 1 cm (½ inch) cubes

300 g (10 oz) spinach, washed and roughly torn

2 tablespoons torn fresh sage leaves

1 teaspoon freshly grated nutmeg

200 g (7 oz) can sweetcorn (preferably without salt or sugar), drained

black pepper

1 Cook the pasta in a large saucepan of boiling water for about 10 minutes until *al dente* – tender but firm to the bite.

2 Meanwhile, prepare the sauce. Melt the butter with the oil in a large frying pan, add the squash and cook for about 6 minutes until softened and slightly browned.

3 Add the spinach, sage, nutmeg and pepper. Cook, stirring, for a further 3 minutes. Add the sweetcorn and heat through.

4 Drain the pasta and add to the pan. Toss well with the sauce and serve.

OKAY FOR UNDER-ONES?
6–12 months If you can't find sweetcorn canned without salt and sugar, use cooked frozen sweetcorn instead. Blend the pasta with a little sauce. Once your baby can chew, cut the pasta up small.

✳ TIP
You can use any other edible squash; even pumpkin, though it's very watery when cooked.

oodles of noodles

Noodles are tricky for children to eat, but many love the challenge of twiddling them around a fork. For very young children, cook pasta twists.

3 SERVINGS

2 teaspoons vegetable oil

½ small onion, finely chopped

1 small garlic clove, crushed

4 tomatoes, skinned, deseeded and chopped

½ courgette, finely diced

125 g (4 oz) dried tagliatelle

25 g (1 oz) frozen peas

1 teaspoon sun-dried tomato paste

2 tablespoons single cream

to serve

Parmesan cheese shavings

1 Heat the oil in a saucepan, add the onion and fry, stirring occasionally, for 4–5 minutes until lightly browned. Stir in the garlic, tomatoes and courgette. Cover and cook gently for 10 minutes, stirring occasionally, to make the sauce.

2 Meanwhile, cook the pasta in a large saucepan of boiling water until *al dente* – tender but firm to the bite.

3 Add the peas and tomato paste to the sauce and cook for 3 minutes, then stir in the cream.

4 Drain the pasta and spoon into bowls. Spoon on the sauce and top with cheese shavings.

OKAY FOR UNDER-ONES?
6–9 months Omit the peas. Purée 1 tablespoon of the sauce and 3 tablespoons of the pasta with a little milk to the required texture. Include a little grated mild Cheddar if liked.

9–12 months Finely chop or mash the food to the desired texture.

✳ TIPS
If preferred, omit the courgette or replace with a little finely diced carrot and red pepper.

A 200 g (7 oz) can of tomatoes could be used instead of fresh ones; break them up with a spoon as the sauce cooks.

cleopatra's rice

Based on an Egyptian favourite, this dish, topped with courgette sticks and creamy bio yogurt, combines lentils with rice for optimum protein.

4 SERVINGS

125 g (4 oz) green lentils, rinsed

1.2 litres (2 pints) homemade vegetable stock (see page 126)

1 teaspoon ground cumin

1 teaspoon ground coriander

1 bay leaf

150 g (5 oz) basmati rice, rinsed

2 tablespoons vegetable oil

1 onion, finely chopped

grated rind and juice of 1 lemon

2 courgettes, about 250 g (8 oz), cut into sticks

1 teaspoon clear honey (optional)

150 g (5 oz) natural bio yogurt

1 tablespoon chopped fresh mint

OKAY FOR UNDER-ONES?
6–9 months Omit the lemon rind, juice, honey and onions. Mash or purée more rice with yogurt and steamed courgette.

9–12 months Omit the honey and fried onions.

1 Put the lentils, 1 litre (1¾ pints) of the stock, the spices and bay leaf into a large saucepan. Bring to the boil, then cover and simmer for 30–40 minutes or until tender, stirring occasionally.

2 Cook the rice separately in boiling water until tender, then drain and rinse with hot water.

3 Heat 1 tablespoon of the oil in a frying pan. Add the onion and fry until golden. Pour off the excess stock from the lentils and reserve. Add the fried onion, rice, lemon rind and juice to the lentils. Cover and set aside until ready to serve.

4 Heat the remaining oil in the cleaned frying pan. Add the courgette and stir-fry for 5 minutes until lightly browned. Drizzle with the honey, if using, and cook for 1 minute.

5 Reheat the lentils, stirring, and moisten with the reserved stock if needed. Pile into serving bowls. Flavour the yogurt with the chopped mint. Spoon the yogurt on top of the lentil mixture and surround with the courgette sticks. Serve with warmed pitta breads.

* TIP
You can freeze this dish – without the courgettes or yogurt – in individual portions for up to six weeks. Reheat in the microwave, but remember to stir well to ensure there are no hot spots.

ippy dippers

Try this oven-baked version of egg and chips for a healthy, fuss-free supper that children will want again and again.

2 SERVINGS

1 baking potato, about 250 g (8 oz), scrubbed

½ parsnip, about 150 g (5 oz), peeled

2 small carrots, about 150 g (5 oz), peeled

3 tablespoons olive oil

pinch of turmeric

pinch of paprika

2 eggs

✳ TIP
Some children may prefer this dish without the parsnip; for more adventurous tastebuds add sweet potato and butternut squash.

OKAY FOR UNDER-ONES?
6–9 months Cook the root vegetables in full-fat cow's milk and purée with well-cooked egg yolk to the desired texture.

9–12 months Finely chop the vegetables and whole egg. Older children can pick up cooled vegetable chips.

1 Cut the potato and parsnip into wedge-shaped chips, about 6 cm (2½ inches) long. Cut the carrots into thick sticks, about the same length. Cook in a saucepan of boiling water for 4 minutes.

2 Meanwhile, heat the oil in a small roasting tin in a preheated oven at 220°C (425°F), Gas Mark 7 for 2 minutes.

3 Drain the vegetables, add to the hot oil and toss to coat. Sprinkle with the spices and roast in the oven for 20 minutes. Turn the vegetables and make a space in the middle of them. Break the eggs into this space and bake for a further 5 minutes until the eggs are well cooked. Serve with homemade tomato ketchup.

beat-the-clock pizzas

These scone-based pizzas are simple to make and shape. Use them to introduce your child to the basics of 'telling the time'.

MAKES 4

250 g (8 oz) self-raising flour

50 g (2 oz) unsalted butter, diced

1 egg

100 ml (3½ fl oz) full-fat milk

4 tablespoons passata

4 teaspoons chopped fresh oregano, marjoram or mixed herbs

50 g (2 oz) frozen sweetcorn

50 g (2 oz) medium Cheddar or mozzarella cheese, grated

to finish

2 green peppers, halved, cored and deseeded

1 red pepper, halved, cored and deseeded

1 Put the flour into a bowl and rub in the butter using your fingertips or an electric mixer until the mixture resembles fine crumbs. Stir in the egg and enough milk to mix to a smooth, soft, but not sticky dough.

2 Knead lightly on a floured surface, then divide the dough into 4 pieces. Roll out each one to a 12 cm (5 inch) circle. Place on a large greased baking sheet and brush with passata. Sprinkle with the herbs and sweetcorn.

3 Top with the grated cheese and bake in a preheated oven at 200°C (400°F), Gas Mark 6 for 10 minutes until well risen and the cheese is melted.

4 Cut the main clock numerals from green pepper, using tiny number cutters. Cut red pepper clock hands. Arrange on the pizzas and serve warm, with cherry tomatoes and sliced cucumber, if liked.

OKAY FOR UNDER-ONES?
6–9 months Not suitable. See pages 46–54 for other suggestions.

9–12 months Cut pizza into small strips. Serve, barely warm, as finger food.

* TIP
To make one large pizza rather than individual ones, shape the dough into a 25 cm (10 inch) circle and bake for 15 minutes.

mini banana castles

These mini sponge puddings with their vibrant raspberry sauce are the perfect ending to a special family meal.

4 SERVINGS

50 g (2 oz) butter

50 g (2 oz) self-raising flour

25 g (1 oz) caster sugar

25 g (1 oz) ground almonds

½ teaspoon baking powder

1 egg

1 small ripe banana

raspberry sauce

250 g (8 oz) frozen raspberries

4 teaspoons icing sugar

✳ TIPS

Strawberries can be used instead of raspberries.

If fresh berries are out of season, use frozen ones or frozen mixed berry fruits.

OKAY FOR UNDER-ONES?

6–12 months Not suitable. Offer mashed banana mixed with unsweetened sieved raspberry purée. Or mix banana with some natural bio yogurt. Chop or mash coarsely for older babies.

---

1 Lightly oil four 150 ml (¼ pint) individual metal pudding moulds and line the bases with rounds of greaseproof paper.

2 Put the butter, flour, sugar, ground almonds and baking powder into a bowl or food processor. Add the egg and beat until smooth. Mash the banana and stir into the mixture. Divide between the prepared moulds and level the surface.

3 Bake in a preheated oven at 180°C (350°F), Gas Mark 4 for 15 minutes until well risen and golden, and the tops spring back when lightly pressed with a fingertip.

4 Meanwhile, make the raspberry sauce. Set aside 75 g (3 oz) of the raspberries. Purée the rest of them and sieve to remove the seeds, then mix with 3 teaspoons of the icing sugar. Spoon on to 4 serving plates.

5 Loosen the puddings from their moulds with a round-bladed knife, then turn out and peel off the lining paper. Stand a pudding on each plate on the pool of sauce. Arrange the reserved raspberries on the sponges and sift the remaining icing sugar over the top to decorate.

creamy raspberry fool

Raspberries are a great treat, with their deep rose colour and intense flavour. Occasionally they are so sweet that extra sugar is unnecessary.

6 SERVINGS

200 g (7 oz) fresh raspberries

2–3 tablespoons icing sugar (preferably unrefined)

5 tablespoons double cream

200 g (7 oz) fromage frais

1 Set aside 25 g (1 oz) of the raspberries. Purée the rest in a blender or food processor, then press through a sieve into a bowl to remove the seeds. Stir in the icing sugar to taste.

✳ TIP
For over-twos you can use half-fat fromage frais.

To make a frozen dessert, freeze this fool in little plastic tubs or ice lolly tubes.

2 Whip the cream in a separate bowl until thickened, then fold in the fromage frais. Add the raspberry purée and beat again until smooth and slightly thickened. Taste for sweetness.

3 Spoon into small serving bowls and chill until required. Scatter with the reserved raspberries to serve.

OKAY FOR UNDER-ONES?
6–12 months Omit the icing sugar. Don't be alarmed to see raspberry pips in your baby's nappy, as they pass through intact.

fruit crumble

A good crumble, with its crunchy top and soft inside, makes a sustaining pudding. Apple and mango is a combination that most children love.

6 SERVINGS

2 large cooking apples

1 mango

juice of 1 lemon

125–150 g (4–5 oz) muscovado sugar

200 g (7 oz) plain flour

1 teaspoon baking powder

25 g (1 oz) ground almonds

75 g (3 oz) unsalted butter, cut into small pieces

25–50 g (1–2 oz) rolled oats

1 Peel, core and slice the apples. Peel and slice the mango, discarding the stone. Mix the fruit with the lemon juice and 25–50 g (1–2 oz) sugar to taste, in a buttered 1.8 litre (3 pint) pie dish.

2 Mix the flour, baking powder and ground almonds together in a large bowl. Add the butter and rub in until the mixture resembles fine crumbs. Stir in 75 g (3 oz) of sugar, plus the oats.

3 Spread the crumble over the fruit and bake in a preheated oven at 180°C (350°F), Gas Mark 4 for about 30 minutes, or until the top is golden . Serve with custard, ice cream or creamy yogurt.

OKAY FOR UNDER-ONES?

6–9 months Give some stewed fruit such as apple, blackcurrants sweetened with a little apple juice or sieved plums. Mash the fruit and serve with yogurt.

9–12 months As above, or cut up small. Alternatively, give pieces of raw apple, pear, mango, or banana as finger foods with yogurt.

✳ TIP
Instead of apple and mango, try apple and blackberry; apple and blackcurrant; or pear and banana – you need 500 g (1 lb) fruit.

fresh fruit salad

Fresh fruit dessert is straightforward to prepare and easy for children to eat. Most fruits are available all year – include a good range in your child's diet.

4 SERVINGS

2 oranges

1 apple, cored and chopped

1 pear, cored and chopped

200 ml (7 fl oz) unsweetened apple juice

1–2 bananas

> *** TIP**
> Choose homegrown fruits when they are in season, as they will be at the peak of their flavour.

OKAY FOR UNDER-ONES?
6–9 months Give some ripe pear, banana, melon, blueberries or mango, mashed with a little fruit juice. Or offer stewed eating apple. When a baby is old enough to suck food, give pieces of fruit to eat with their fingers.

9–12 months When your baby can chew, cut fruit up and mix with a little juice.

1 Peel and segment 1 orange; squeeze the juice from the other. Put all the ingredients, except the banana, in a large bowl and toss to mix.

2 Slice the banana and add to the fruit salad just before serving, otherwise it will discolour. Toss to mix.

3 Serve the fruit with yogurt, crème fraîche or ice cream.

VARIATIONS

Melon and blueberry salad
Quarter, deseed, peel and chop 1 small melon. Toss with 175 g (6 oz) fresh blueberries in 300 ml (½ pint) apple juice.

Mango and banana salad
Peel and chop 2 ripe mangoes, cutting the flesh away from the stones. Toss the chopped mango with 2 sliced bananas in 300 ml (½ pint) apple and mango juice.

Pear, raspberry and kiwifruit salad
Core and slice 2 fresh ripe pears and mix with 175 g (6 oz) raspberries, 2 sliced kiwifruit and 300 ml (½ pint) fruit juice, such as apple and pear, apple and raspberry, red grape or pineapple.

dreamy dunkers

This recipe will tempt those children who are reluctant to eat fruit. You can make the sauce in advance, but prepare the fruits at the last minute.

4 SERVINGS

chocolate sauce

125 g (5 oz) good-quality milk chocolate, in pieces

75 ml (3 fl oz) full-fat milk

2 teaspoons golden syrup

dunkers

1 red-skinned apple, cored

2 peaches, stoned

1 kiwifruit, peeled

250 g (8 oz) strawberries

1 banana, peeled

> **✳ TIP**
> Serve chocolate sauce with fruit-filled pancakes, or with bananas and ice cream.

OKAY FOR UNDER-ONES?
6–9 months Purée or mash some peach with a few strawberries, then sieve. Stir in natural bio yogurt – offer tiny first tastes.

9–12 months Serve without the chocolate sauce.

1 Put the chocolate into a small saucepan with the milk and golden syrup. Heat gently, stirring occasionally, until melted and smooth. Pour the chocolate sauce into 4 small dishes and set each one on a larger individual serving plate.

2 Cut the apple, peaches and kiwifruit into chunks. Halve or quarter the strawberries. Thickly slice the banana. Arrange the fruit on the serving plates. Provide small forks to enable children to dunk the fruits into the warm sauce.

VARIATION
Strawberry fondue
Purée 100 g (3½ oz) strawberries, sieve to remove seeds, then stir into 200 g (7 oz) Greek yogurt. Sweeten with 1–2 teaspoons caster sugar if required. Serve with fruits for dipping, as above.

pink blush jellies

Packets of jelly invariably include artificial flavourings and colourings. These fruit jellies are a natural vitamin C-packed, low-sugar dessert.

4 SERVINGS

125 g (4 oz) redcurrants

250 ml (8 fl oz) water

100 g (3½ oz) strawberries

75 g (3 oz) seedless red grapes, halved

300 ml (½ pint) unsweetened apple juice

1 sachet gelatine

50 g (2 oz) caster sugar

* TIPS
If preferred, 1 sliced small banana can be used in place of the strawberries.

During the winter months, use frozen mixed soft fruits in place of the redcurrants and strawberries.

For children who hate bits, purée the fruits and stir into the jelly.

OKAY FOR UNDER-ONES?
6–12 months Not suitable. See pages 72–73 for other ideas.

1 Rinse the redcurrants and put into a saucepan with the water. Bring to the boil and simmer for 5 minutes. Press through a sieve to remove skins.

2 Divide the strawberries and grapes between four 150 ml (¼ pint) individual jelly moulds.

3 Pour the apple juice into a saucepan, sprinkle in the gelatine and stir until dissolved, then add the redcurrant juice and sugar. Bring to the boil, stirring, until thickened, then pour straight into the jelly moulds. Allow to cool, then refrigerate for 2–3 hours until set.

4 To turn each jelly out, briefly dip the mould into a bowl of very hot water. Loosen the edges with your fingertips and invert the mould on to a plate. Holding the mould and plate together, jerk to release the jelly, then serve.

iced mango yogurt

This creamy, fruity yogurt makes a light, refreshing pudding or between-meal treat. Mangoes are ready to eat if they give slightly when pressed.

8 SERVINGS

100 g (3½ oz) caster sugar

75 ml (3 fl oz) water

2 ripe mangoes

juice of 1 lemon

500 ml (17 fl oz) Greek yogurt

* TIPS

If you don't have fresh mangoes, use canned mangoes or ripe pears.

This mixture can be used to make ice lollies for older children. After whisking the partially frozen yogurt ice, pack into 8–10 plastic lolly moulds and freeze overnight until firm. Briefly hold under hot water to unmould.

OKAY FOR UNDER-ONES?
6–12 months Although not totally unsuitable, it's better not to give babies foods with added sugar. Instead, give some puréed mango mixed with yogurt.

1 Put the sugar and water in a small heavy-based saucepan and heat gently until the sugar dissolves. Leave to cool.

2 Halve, stone and peel the mangoes. Cut the flesh up roughly and place in a food processor or blender. Add the lemon juice and blend until smooth, then turn into a bowl.

3 Add the cooled syrup and yogurt to the mango purée and beat well. Transfer to a shallow plastic container and freeze until thickened around the edges, which should take about 2 hours.

4 Turn the mixture into a bowl and whisk until smooth and thickened. Return to the freezer container. Cover and freeze for at least 2 hours, or overnight until firm.

5 Transfer to the refrigerator about 30 minutes before serving to soften slightly. Serve the iced yogurt on its own or with a fresh fruit salad (see page 112).

fruit smoothies

These fruit-enriched drinks – based on milk, yogurt or soft cheese – are tempting and highly nutritious. Serve as a healthy snack or dessert.

EACH SERVES 2

100 g (3½ oz) raspberries, defrosted if frozen

2 ripe peaches, halved, stoned and roughly chopped

4 tablespoons fromage frais

200 ml (7 fl oz) full-fat milk

✳ TIPS

Experiment with your own combinations of fruit and milk, yogurt or soft cheese.

Young children can help make smoothies by measuring the ingredients.

OKAY FOR UNDER-ONES?
Do not give smoothies that contain ice cream or sugar to under-ones.

6–9 months Reduce the amount of milk and serve as a pudding.

9–12 months Dilute drinks with extra milk so that they will go through the holes in a feeder beaker, or offer from an open cup.

1 Put the raspberries, peaches, fromage frais and milk into a blender or food processor and process until smooth.

2 Sieve to remove the pips, then pour into two glasses. Serve with straws.

VARIATIONS

Strawberry crush
Purée and sieve 100 g (3½ oz) strawberries. Whisk with 200 g (7 oz) Greek yogurt and 200 ml (7 fl oz) full-fat milk. Sweeten with a little caster sugar if required. Pour into tall glasses and top with strawberry slices.

Apricot smoothie
Tip a 411 g (13½ oz) can apricot halves in natural juice into a blender or food processor. Add 100 g (3½ oz) ricotta cheese and process until smooth. Pour into glasses and serve with straws.

Banana and chocolate duet
Put 2 thickly sliced small bananas, 2 scoops chocolate ice cream and 300 ml (½ pint) full-fat milk into a blender or food processor and blend until smooth and frothy. Pour into glasses and top with a sprinkling of grated chocolate or drinking chocolate powder.

chocolate crumbles

These delectable chocolate cookies need little extra sugar. They are also packed with oats and wholemeal flour, for a good source of lasting energy.

MAKES 16–20

125 g (4 oz) plain wholemeal flour

1 teaspoon baking powder

125 g (4 oz) porridge oats

125 g (4 oz) unsalted butter, melted and cooled slightly

40 g (1½ oz) light muscovado sugar

1 egg, beaten

150 g (5 oz) good-quality plain, milk or white chocolate, in small pieces

1 Mix the flour, baking powder and oats together in a bowl. Add the butter, sugar, egg and chocolate and beat until evenly combined.

2 Take dessertspoonfuls of the mixture and pat roughly into cakes. Place slightly apart on a greased large baking sheet.

3 Bake in a preheated oven at 200°C (400°F), Gas Mark 6 for about 15 minutes until slightly risen and lightly coloured. Leave on the baking sheet for 2 minutes, then cool on a wire rack.

4 Store in an airtight container for up to 4 days. Serve as a snack, or with some raspberries or strawberries and fromage frais as a dessert.

OKAY FOR UNDER-ONES?
6–9 months Not suitable.

9–12 months It's best not to give under-ones food with added sugar, and that includes chocolate. However, the occasional cookie – perhaps once a week – won't hurt an older baby, provided the teeth and gums are cleaned afterwards.

* TIPS
For an extra chocolatey flavour, use dark chocolate that contains a minimum of 70% cocoa solids.

Butter and chocolate are high in saturated fat, so discourage older children from pigging out on these cookies; if they do, cut down on the fat – and saturated fat in particular – they have for the rest of the day.

oat and apple muffins

Muffins are easy to make and are a great teatime treat. They're also very good served warm for breakfast – microwave for about 20 seconds.

MAKES 12

125 g (4 oz) plain white flour

125 g (4 oz) wholemeal plain flour

1 tablespoon baking powder

50 g (2 oz) medium oatmeal

50 g (2 oz) light muscovado sugar

3 small dessert apples, peeled, cored and diced

50 g (2 oz) sultanas or raisins

50 g (2 oz) unsalted butter, melted and cooled slightly

150 ml (¼ pint) yogurt

150 ml (¼ pint) full-fat milk

1 egg

5 tablespoons clear honey

a little extra oatmeal, for dusting

OKAY FOR UNDER-ONES?
6–9 months Not suitable.

9–12 months The occasional muffin won't hurt an older baby, provided teeth and gums are cleaned soon after. Use double the amount of sugar instead of honey.

1 Line a 12-hole muffin tray or deep bun tin with paper muffin cases. Mix the flours, baking powder, oatmeal and sugar in a bowl. Stir in the chopped apples and sultanas or raisins.

2 In another bowl, beat together the butter, yogurt, milk, egg and honey. Add this mixture to the dry ingredients and stir quickly and briefly, until just incorporated; do not over-mix.

3 Divide the mixture between the paper cases and sprinkle with a little extra oatmeal. Bake in a preheated oven at 200°C (400°F), Gas Mark 6 for 18–20 minutes until just firm to the touch. Transfer to a wire rack to cool.

4 Serve warm or cold with stewed apple or plums, for a tasty dessert.

flapjacks

Flapjacks are always popular and this version with its hint of warm ginger and moist, chewy dried fruit is especially good.

MAKES 20

50 g (2 oz) unsalted butter

75 g (3 oz) muscovado sugar

1 teaspoon powdered ginger (optional)

4 tablespoons vegetable oil

250 g (8 oz) rolled oats

25 g (1 oz) sultanas

50 g (2 oz) chopped dried apricots, papaya, pears or peaches (or a mixture)

> **✳ TIP**
> Flapjacks keep well in an airtight tin, or they can be frozen.

OKAY FOR UNDER-ONES?
6–9 months Not suitable. Give mashed stewed apricot or eating apple, or mashed banana, ripe peach or pear, moistened with a little apple juice.

9–12 months Offer fruit or, for older babies give baked bread rusks, toast soldiers or crumpet fingers.

1 Line a 30 x 20 cm (12 x 8 inch) Swiss roll tin with non-stick baking paper.

2 Put the butter and sugar in a large saucepan and heat gently until melted, then stir in the ginger, if using, and oil. Add the oats, sultanas and fruit, and stir to mix.

3 Spoon the mixture into the prepared tin, level the surface and press down gently. Bake in a preheated oven at 180°C (350°F), Gas Mark 4 for 30 minutes. Leave in the tin for 10 minutes, then cut into slices. Leave until cold before removing from the tin.

4 Serve flapjacks on their own, or with stewed apple or plums as a dessert.

banana teabread

This moist, fragrant teabread is perfect for a mid-morning break or at teatime. Muscovado sugar and wholemeal flour make a healthier cake.

MAKES 10–12 SLICES

200 g (7 oz) self-raising wholemeal flour

1 teaspoon bicarbonate of soda

½ teaspoon ground mixed spice

75 g (3 oz) muscovado sugar

2 bananas

4 tablespoons rapeseed (canola) oil

2 eggs, beaten

4 tablespoons full-fat milk

2 teaspoons vanilla extract

40 g (1½ oz) dried banana chips

OKAY FOR UNDER-ONES?
Not suitable – self-raising flour and bicarbonate of soda contain sodium.

6–9 months Give mashed stewed apricot or eating apple, or mashed banana, ripe peach or pear.

9–12 months Offer one of the above alternatives or, for older babies who can chew, give baked bread rusks, toast soldiers or crumpet fingers.

1 Line a 23 x 12 cm (9 x 5 inch) loaf tin with non-stick baking paper. Combine the flour, bicarbonate of soda, mixed spice and sugar in a large bowl and make a well in the centre. Mash the bananas and add to the well with the oil, eggs, milk and vanilla extract. Stir. Put the mixture into the loaf tin and smooth the top. Chop the dried banana chips and sprinkle over the surface of the mixture.

2 Bake in a preheated oven at 180°C (350°F), Gas Mark 4 for 45–50 minutes, or until the loaf is well risen, firm to the touch, and a skewer inserted into the middle comes out clean. Leave to cool then serve in slices.

✳ TIP
Mash the bananas just before incorporating them into the mixture, otherwise the flesh will turn black as it is oxidized by the air.

carrot cakes

One way to ensure that your children eat enough vegetables and fruit is to incorporate them into as many recipes as you can.

MAKES 10

175 g (6 oz) self-raising wholemeal flour

125 g (4 oz) muscovado sugar

2 teaspoons baking powder

1 teaspoon ground cinnamon

pinch of ground nutmeg

3 eggs, beaten

150 ml (¼ pint) rapeseed oil

1 teaspoon vanilla extract

250 g (8 oz) peeled carrots, grated

frosting (optional)
75 g (3 oz) cream cheese

1 teaspoon vanilla extract

50 g (2 oz) icing sugar

1 Put the flour, sugar, baking powder, cinnamon and nutmeg into a large bowl, stir to mix, then make a well in the centre. Stir in the eggs, oil, vanilla extract and carrots.

2 Line 10 sections of a 12-hole muffin tray with paper cases, and spoon the mixture into the cases. Bake in a preheated oven at 180°C (350°F), Gas Mark 4 for 25–30 minutes, until well risen and golden brown. Cool on a wire rack.

3 To make the frosting, if required, mix the ingredients together in a bowl until smooth then swirl a teaspoonful of frosting on to the top of each cake. Serve the cakes on their own, or as a dessert with Greek yogurt.

OKAY FOR UNDER-ONES?
Not suitable – contains added sugar and self-raising flour and baking powder contain sodium.

6–9 months Offer mashed or chopped ripe pear or stewed eating apple.

9–12 months Give chopped ripe pear or toast soldiers.

✳ TIP
Take the time to make the cream cheese frosting as it adds extra visual appeal.

animal magic

Children enjoy making these as much as they love to eat them. Choose simple shaped cutters – tiny ears or tails can be difficult to turn out.

MAKES 16

75 g (3 oz) unsalted butter or margarine

3 tablespoons golden syrup

200 g (7 oz) bar good-quality plain chocolate, in pieces

100 g (3½ oz) Rice Krispies

50 g (2 oz) good-quality white chocolate, in pieces

✳ TIPS

If you do not have enough animal cutters, spoon the remaining mixture into paper cases.

For shape-sorter cakes press the mixture into an oiled 30 x 20 x 4 cm (12 x 8 x 1½ inch) cake tin or foil-lined baking tin. Chill and cut into squares, triangles or rounds.

OKAY FOR UNDER-ONES?
6–12 months Not suitable. See pages 55–56 and 72–73 for alternatives.

1 Brush 16 animal biscuit cutters with oil and place on a large oiled baking sheet.

2 Put the butter, syrup and plain chocolate in a saucepan and heat gently, stirring occasionally, until melted. Take off the heat and add the cereal, stirring to ensure it is well coated in chocolate.

3 Spoon the chocolate mixture into the animal cutters and press the mixture down well. Chill until firm. Free the edges of the biscuits with a small knife or by flexing the cutters and remove.

4 Melt the white chocolate in a heatproof bowl over a saucepan of simmering water, then spoon into a greaseproof paper piping bag and snip off the tip. Use to pipe features on to the animals and leave to harden for 30 minutes before serving.

brownies

Luscious chocolate brownies are an irresistible treat. Most children like them without nuts, though added chunks of white chocolate are popular.

MAKES 20

50 g (2 oz) unsalted butter

2 tablespoons vegetable oil

2 eggs, beaten

125 g (4 oz) muscovado sugar

1 teaspoon vanilla extract

125 g (4 oz) self-raising flour

40 g (1½ oz) cocoa powder

50 g (2 oz) ground hazelnuts (optional)

* TIP
Brownies freeze well, but make double the quantity as your family will probably devour them before they reach the freezer.

OKAY FOR UNDER-ONES?
Not suitable – self-raising flour contains sodium.

6–9 months Give mashed stewed apricot or apple, pear or raw cherries.

9–12 months Offer fruit or baked bread rusks.

1 Line a 20 cm (8 inch) square cake tin with non-stick baking paper.

2 Melt the butter in a large saucepan over a low heat. Remove from the heat and mix in the oil, eggs, sugar and vanilla extract. Then stir in the flour and cocoa powder, followed by the ground hazelnuts, if using.

3 Bake in a preheated oven at 180°C (350°F), Gas Mark 4 for 30 minutes. Remove from the oven, leave to stand for 10 minutes, then cut into squares. Allow the brownies to cool completely before removing from the tin.

4 Serve brownies on their own, or with creamy natural yogurt as a dessert.

stock recipes

There is no need to make stocks yourself if you are pressed for time: however, the flavour is much better than shop-bought equivalents. Commercial brands are often very salty.

vegetable stock

1.8 LITRES (3 PINTS)

1.8 litres (3 pints) water

1 onion, unpeeled and halved

1 garlic clove, unpeeled and halved

1 carrot, roughly chopped

1 celery stick with leaves, roughly chopped

1 leek, roughly chopped

peelings of 1–2 scrubbed potatoes

1 bay leaf

1 parsley sprig

1 Combine the measured water with all the remaining ingredients in a deep saucepan. Bring to the boil, then lower the heat and simmer for 2½–3 hours.

2 Cool, then strain through a sieve, discarding all the vegetables and herbs in the sieve. Store the stock in the refrigerator. Use within 3–4 days, or, if frozen, within 4 months.

chicken stock

ABOUT 3.6 LITRES (6 PINTS)

1 whole chicken carcass

3.6 litres (6 pints) water

1 teaspoon salt

1 onion, peeled

2 celery sticks, chopped

2 carrots, roughly chopped

2 parsley sprigs

1 bay leaf

1 Put the carcass into a deep saucepan, cover with water and add the salt. Bring to the boil and simmer for 1 hour.

2 Add the vegetables and herbs and simmer for a further 1½–2 hours. Add more water if necessary.

3 Remove the carcass and strain the stock into a bowl, discarding the vegetables and herbs.

4 Leave the cool, then skim off the fat with a spoon. Store in the refrigerator and use within 3 days, or, if frozen, within 3 months.

index

acknowledgements

Getty Images 7
Octopus Publishing Group Limited 3, 29, 31
top right, 31 centre right top, 31 centre right
bottom, 70, 77, 81, 83, 86, 89, 91, 93, 95, 102,
110, 111, 113, 119, 120, 121, 122, 125;/Frank
Adam 15 bottom left;/David Jordan 1, 13 top
right, 13 bottom right, 13 bottom left, 13
bottom centre, 20 bottom right, 25, 31 bottom
right, 33, 40, 42, 47, 49, 51, 52, 54, 57, 59, 63, 64,
66, 67, 68, 71, 97, 98, 100, 105, 106, 109, 114,
115;/Sandra Lane 15 bottom centre left;/William
Lingwood 15 bottom centre right, 21 bottom
centre;/Sean Myers 15 bottom right;/Peter
Pugh-Cook 9, 11, 35 top right, 35 bottom
right;/William Reavell 8, 20 top left;/Craig
Robertson 21 bottom right;/Russell Sadur 2, 12

Executive Editor **Nicola Hill**
Project Editor **Kate Tuckett**
Executive Art Editor **Rozelle Bentheim**
Designer **Lisa Tai**
Production Controller **Nosheen Shan**